MEL BAY'S COMPLETE 7-STRING GUITAR METHOD

A Comprehensive Method Including Chords, Scales & Arpeggios

BY CHRIS BUZZELLI

Online Audio Tracks

1 Tuning to the recording [1:32]
2 Playalong Exercise #1, #2, #6, #7, #8 [3:28]
3 Playalong Exercise #3, #9, #10 [3:19]
4 Playalong Exercise #4, #12, #13, #20 [3:14]
5 Playalong Exercise #5, #11 [3:54]
6 Playalong Exercise #14 [1:52]
7 Playalong Exercise #15 [1:48]
8 Playalong Exercise #16 [3:18]
9 Playalong Exercise #17 [3:17]
10 Playalong Exercise #18 [3:19]
11 Playalong Exercise #19 [3:11]
12 Playalong Exercise #21 [3:18]
13 Playalong Exercise #22 [3:13]

14 Study No. 1 [0:30]
15 Study No. 2 [0:29]
16 Study No. 3 [0:29]
17 Study No. 4 [0:27]
18 Study No. 5 [0:23]
19 Study No. 6 [0:35]
20 Study No. 7 [0:24]
21 Study No. 8 [0:32]
22 Study No. 9 [0:27]
23 Study No. 10 [0:25]
24 Study No. 11 [0:24]
25 Study No. 12 [0:27]
26 Study No. 13 [0:32]
27 Study No. 14 [0:38]
28 Study No. 15 [0:24]

29 Study No. 16 [0:28]
30 Study No. 17 [:28]
31 Study No. 18 [0:32]
32 Study No. 19 [0:37]
33 Study No. 20 [0:31]
34 Study No. 21 [0:23]
35 Study No. 22 [:18]
36 Study No. 23 [0:38]
37 Study No. 24 [0:29]
38 Study No. 25 [0:21]
39 Study No. 26 [0:32]
40 Study No. 27 [0:41]
41 Study No. 28 [0:25]
42 Study No. 29 [0:26]
43 Study No. 30 [0:33]

"This book is a 'must have' for anyone interested in the 7 string guitar."

Jimmy Bruno

"Chris' book is a valuable and much needed addition to the literature available to the seven string guitarist-a thorough study and expansion of the fundamentals that will give the player both a solid understanding of the instrument's possibilities and well-rounded technical mastery."

Howard Alden

The guitars pictured on the cover are a seven string American Archtop made by Dale Unger and a custom seven string classical guitar made for Chris Buzzelli by Gary Zimnicki.

Cover photo by Rick Luettke.

Online Audio

To access the online audio go to:
www.melbay.com/99988BCDEB

Visit us on the Web at www.melbay.com — E-mail us at email@melbay.com

Contents

Chris Buzzelli

Photo of Chris Buzzelli by Norman Wilson

Chris Buzzelli has been called "a gifted guitarist who deserves to be better known" by Adrian Ingram in <u>Just Jazz Guitar</u> magazine. Jim Fisch, of <u>20th Century Guitar</u>, called his first CD, "What Goes Around", "...superb," while Dave McElfresh, of <u>Cadence</u> magazine said he was "...equally skillful on electric and nylon string guitar, with his exceptional sense of melody and harmony".

A graduate of the University of North Texas, Buzzelli was a recipient of scholarships in both jazz and classical guitar and a member of the prestigious One O'clock Lab Band. His teachers have included Jack Petersen, Dennis Sandole, Joe Pass, Alice Artzt and Sharon Isbin. He has served on the faculties of Bowling Green State University and the University of Michigan. He has written articles for <u>Jazz Educators Journal</u>, <u>Just Jazz Guitar</u>, and <u>American String Teacher</u>, and has a number of transcribed solos, arrangements, and guitar ensemble compositions published by Mel Bay Publications. He has recorded for several different labels as both a leader and a sideman. An active performer, Buzzelli has performed with artists such as Bucky Pizzarelli, Joe Pass, Herb Ellis, Cal Collins, Mike Stern, Tal Farlow, Jack Wilkins, Randy Johnston, Joshua Breakstone, Mark Elf, Frank Vignola and Gene Bertoncini, and has performed in some nationally recognized venues including the Classic American Guitar Show in Long Island, New York and the Chet Atkins Appreciation Society event held each summer in Nashville. For more information, visit ChrisBuzzelli.com.

This book is dedicated to George Van Eps, without whose creativity and imagination, a book such as this one would never have been possible. And, to Jack Petersen, who taught me, among other things, how to approach learning the guitar.

Introduction to the Seven-String Guitar

Why a seven-string guitar?

Aren't six strings hard enough? Of course, they are. You can obviously make a lot of great music on a six-string guitar. Early in the 20th century, the four-string guitar and the four-string banjo were very popular and a lot of music has been played on those instruments as well. Having only four strings doesn't seem to bother violinists or cellists either, and there's certainly nothing easy about those instruments. Still, you don't see many six-string guitarists cutting off two strings because "four are hard enough." To ask this question is really missing the point of the seven-string guitar. The seven-string guitar is simply an enhancement of the six string guitar. Not only does it give the instrument some extra range (which is handy for walking bass lines, etc.), but it will allow you to play chords with a greater "spread." One can play a low "F" and a high "E" on a six-string guitar, but not at the same time. On a seven-string guitar, this can be done easily. Whether or not the seven-string guitar is for you depends on the type of playing you like to do. Most guitarists who play seven-string will tend to use it in any musical setting. Remember, there is virtually nothing you can play on a six-string that you can't play on a seven-string. But, the seven string really shines as a solo instrument, in duos, with other guitarists, vocalists, or other instruments, and even larger groups without a bass. So, if you enjoy playing in this type of setting, or hope to in the future, then seven-string guitar might be for you.

About this book:

This book is designed for guitarists who already play six-string guitar but have an interest in delving into the increasingly popular and satisfying world of the seven-string guitar. It is geared toward the intermediate to advanced student. Those who already have an understanding of scale and chord construction, and other basics of jazz guitar playing, will probably benefit the most from this book. In order to offer the most comprehensive view possible of the seven string guitar, only topics that are unique to the seven string guitar will be covered. Any student that needs a more general approach should consult Mel Bay's Complete Jazz Guitar Method by Mike Christiansen, or one of the other jazz guitar books offered by Mel Bay Publications. The book will be divided into three parts: Part One will cover scales, Part Two arpeggios, and Part Three chord voicings. The parts may be studied in any order, or concurrently, but within each part, the chapters should be taken in order as each chapter will build on the previous ones. While examples and diagrams will be numerous, no attempt will be made to provide every possible scale fingering, arpeggio fingering, or chord voicing, as that would fill many books the size of this one. Instead, the most common and useful examples will be provided along with a clear and concise explanation so that the student can apply the concepts presented here in whatever directions they choose.

About the tuning:

The tuning used throughout this book is that of a standard six-string guitar tuning, with the addition of a low "A" string (an octave below the fifth string). This is the tuning that is, by far, the most popular among seven-string jazz guitarists. It is used by Bucky Pizzarelli, Howard Alden, Jimmy Bruno, Ron Escheté, Fred Fried, many others, and the father of all seven string jazz guitarists, George Van Eps. Actually, later in his career, Van Eps tuned his guitar a step low, but the string relationships were the same, so all of the fingerings and diagrams in this book would still apply to his tuning, but the pitches would be a step lower.

About the notation:

Standard guitar notation, with the addition of two ledger lines below the staff, will be used throughout this book. While some publications use a type of "short hand" to avoid the extra ledger lines, and this works well in some applications, it is not suited to some of the material contained here. Particularly, for some chord voicings, where the seventh string and the fifth string are used simultaneously, the clearest way to notate this is to use the extra ledger lines. Guitarists should already be accustomed to reading three ledger lines below the staff. If you've ever played a piece in "drop-D" tuning, make that four ledger lines. So now, we'll just be adding one more ledger line. I'm sure you can handle that!

Part One - Scales

Introduction to Scales

’m sure that if you are reading this book, then scales are nothing new to you. However, there are a few points that need to be made before we get into the actual fingerings. Scale practice is an accepted and time tested method for musicians to build technique on their instruments. While this alone would be reason enough to learn your scales, improvisers get another important benefit. From scales, we build chords, so the relationship between scales and chords is an important one for an improvising musician to understand. Here is where, if you have only practiced scales in a "traditional" way, you might benefit by thinking of your scales a little differently. Traditionally, scales are practiced by starting on the tonic (otherwise known as the root, or simply the "letter name" of the scale), and playing up the scale stepwise until you reach another root up an octave or two, then playing down the scale stepwise until you get back to the note you started on. While this is a good place to start, if you only practice in this manner, then your solos are likely to sound too "scale-like." Think of your scales as a collection of notes that creates a certain sound, or mood when played against a particular chord. This set of notes can be rearranged an infinite number of ways to generate melodies. Practicing in this way is certainly not the end of the road to becoming an improviser. There are a great many other factors that come into play, like motivic development, use of chromaticism, jazz "vocabulary," etc. These concepts are probably best learned through listening, transcribing and other means. Scale practice, should rather be looked at as a good beginning which will help you develop your "chops," your ear, and your knowledge of the fretboard. With this idea in mind, here are some ways of practicing scales (all shown on a C major scale for demonstration purposes).

Ex. 1 Ascending 3rds:

Ex. 2 Descending 3rds:

Ex. 3 Ascending and descending 3rds:

Ex. 4 Ascending 4ths:

You get the idea. You can do any interval (5ths, 6ths, etc.) ascending, descending, or some combination of the two.

Ex. 5 Ascending triad shapes:

Ex. 6 Descending triad shapes:

Ex. 7 Ascending and descending triad shapes:

Ex. 8 Ascending seventh chord shapes:

Again, you can make up more patterns by playing seventh chords in different directions.

Ex. 9 Mixed scale and arpeggio patterns:

Any kind of pattern you can think of, transposed diatonically to each scale degree.

Ex. 10

Ex. 11

Ex. 12

B e sure as you learn the scales presented in this section, that you understand how each scale can be applied to a particular chord or chord progression. Once you have learned the basic fingering(s), practice the scale with the playalong CD using some of the patterns above, or any others you like, to create different melodies.

A s for the fingerings, keep in mind that they are only suggestions, and you may alter them to suit your own playing style. Each fingering will be presented in three forms: fingerboard diagrams, standard music notation and TAB. I have tried to use fingerings that generally fit under the hand with a minimum of stretches. You will notice that seven string scale fingerings cover a little more fretboard "real estate" than do six-string scale fingerings. Because of the tuning of the lowest two strings, many fingerings have a built-in shift in the lowest octave. Also, to help you become accustomed to the unusual tuning of the bottom two strings, I have included an example of a two-string fingering for each scale. Practicing the scale in this manner will help you integrate the seventh string into your playing. You should also experiment with playing the scale starting on different pitches, but always staying on the bottom two strings.

A fter the play-alongs in each chapter, you will find one or more brief studies that demonstrate the use of the scale. The studies are written in the lower register to make use of the seventh string and to help you get accustomed to this part of the instrument. They do not stay in any one position, and so will also help you see how to connect the position fingerings horizontally.

Major Scales

Major scales are the most fundamental, but also the most useful scales to a jazz musician. Almost all "standard" tunes make use of major scale harmony in some way (even the one's in minor keys!). From a C major scale, the following seventh chords can be built: Cmaj7, Dmi7, Emi7, Fmaj7, G7, Ami7 and Bmi7♭5. So, to some extent, the notes of the C major scale (in whatever order you choose to play them), will fit any one of these chords. Some notes, of course, will be more dissonant than others with a particular chord and might best be used only in passing.

Notice that the individual fingerings have been labeled according to the note that they "start on" (of course, once you are familiar with the fingering, you can start on whatever note you wish). I find that this works better than learning each fingering according to it's modal name. While the use of modes in jazz improvisation has it's place, it is a more advanced concept than the application of major scales. The beginning to intermediate student is better served by first learning the fingerings which are to follow as major scales and dealing with the modal applications at a later time. A brief explanation of modes will appear later in this chapter.

Familiarize yourself with the following fingerings. If you already know your major scales on the six-string guitar, you will simply be adding a few notes to the bottom of the scale. You will find that the seven-string fingerings usually include one or two "shifts" to accommodate the tuning of the low A. Once you are comfortable in the key of C, transpose the fingerings to all of the other major keys. The first fingering starts on the root, so to transpose it, simply be sure that the first note of the fingering is the tonic note of the scale you wish to play. In other words, to use this fingering as an F major scale, start it on an F. To use this fingering as a B♭ major scale, start it on a B♭, etc.

Starts on root

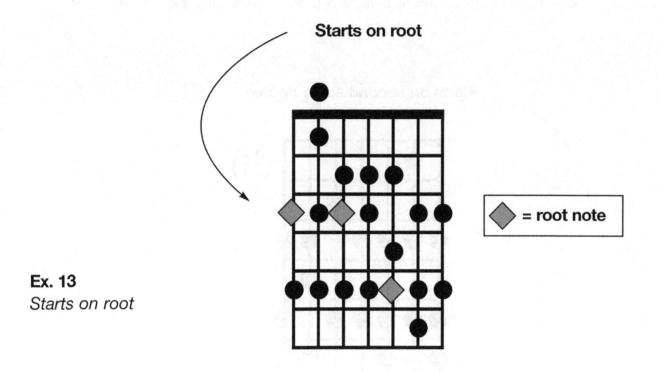

= root note

Ex. 13
Starts on root

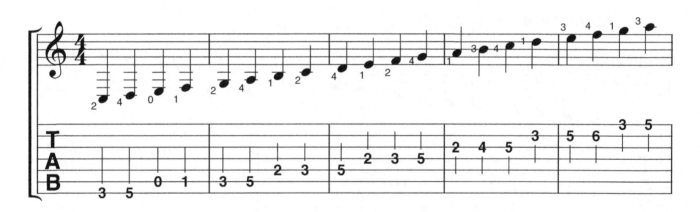

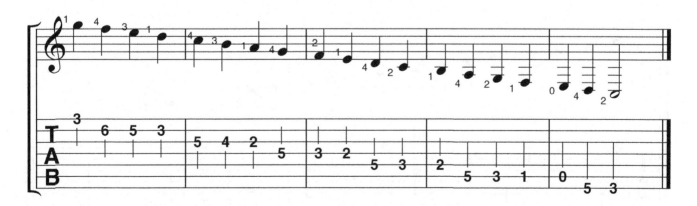

Part one - major scales

This fingering starts on the second scale degree, so to transpose it, be sure that the first note of the fingering is the second note of the scale you wish to play. In other words, to use this fingering as an F major scale, start it on a G. To use this fingering as a B♭ major scale, start it on a C, etc.

Starts on second scale degree

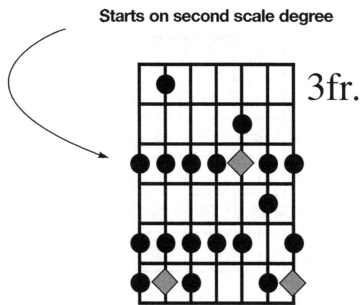

Ex. 14

Starts on second scale degree

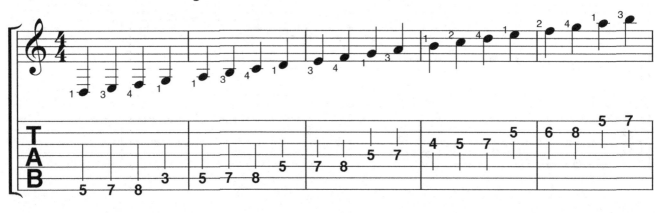

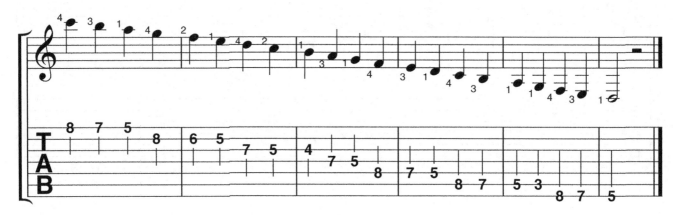

This fingering starts on the third scale degree, so to transpose it, be sure that the first note of the fingering is the third note of the scale you wish to play. In other words, to use this fingering as an F major scale, start it on an A. To use this fingering as a B♭ major scale, start it on a D, etc.

Starts on third scale degree

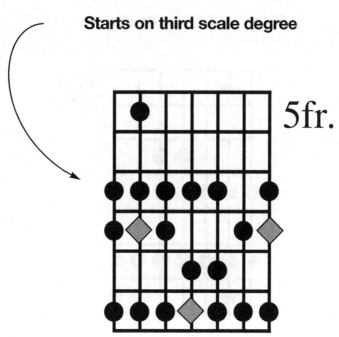

Ex. 15

Starts on third scale degree

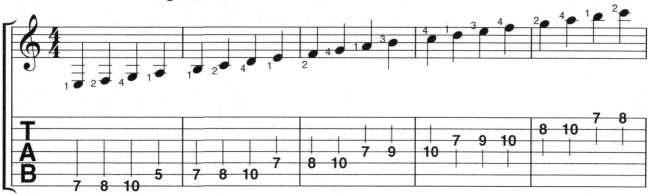

This fingering starts on the fifth scale degree, so to transpose it, be sure that the first note of the fingering is the fifth note of the scale you wish to play. In other words, to use this fingering as an F major scale, start it on a C. To use this fingering as a B♭ major scale, start it on an F, etc.

Starts on fifth scale degree

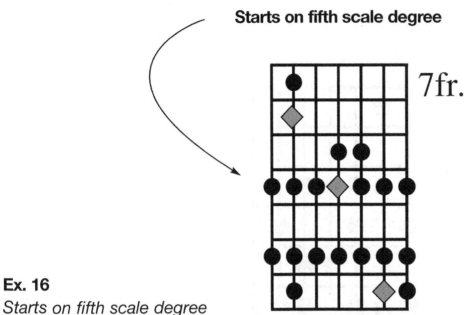

7fr.

Ex. 16

Starts on fifth scale degree

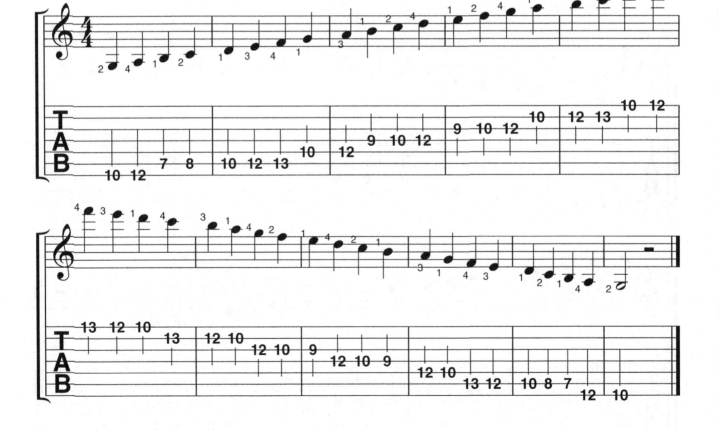

This fingering starts on the sixth scale degree, so to transpose it, be sure that the first note of the fingering is the sixth note of the scale you wish to play. In other words, to use this fingering as an F major scale, start it on a D. To use this fingering as a B♭ major scale, start it on a G, etc.

Starts on sixth scale degree

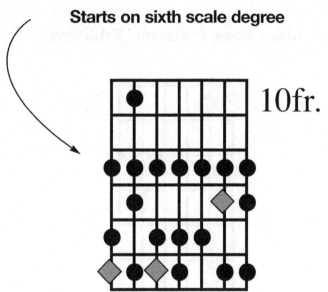

10fr.

Ex. 17

Starts on sixth scale degree

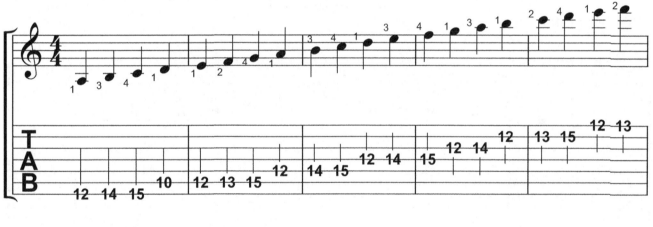

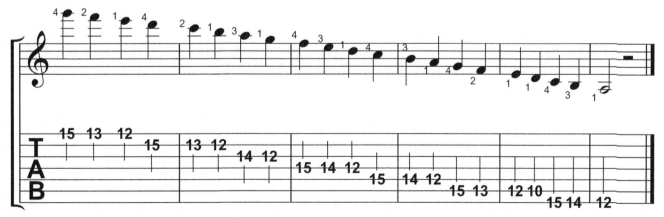

Part one - major scales

Here is a horizontal fingering for a major scale which stays on the bottom two strings. This one goes from root to root, but you should experiment with starting and ending on different notes. There are many ways this could be fingered, so keep in mind that this is only one example.

Major Scale Horizontal Fingering

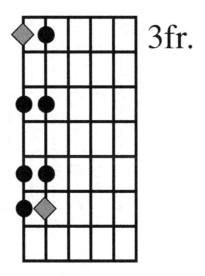

3fr.

Ex. 18
Horizontal Fingering

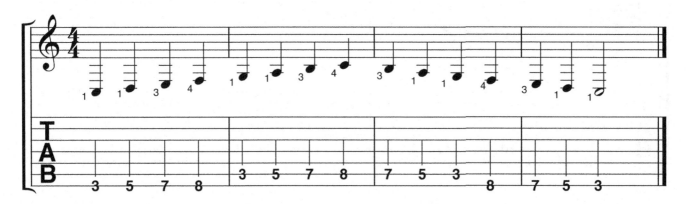

Notice how this horizontal fingering is the same as the first octave of the "starts on 2nd" fingering shown in example 14, except with the addition of the low C.

By combining the horizontal fingering with the "starts on second" fingering, we get a full three-octave C major scale.

Ex. 19
Three octave major scale

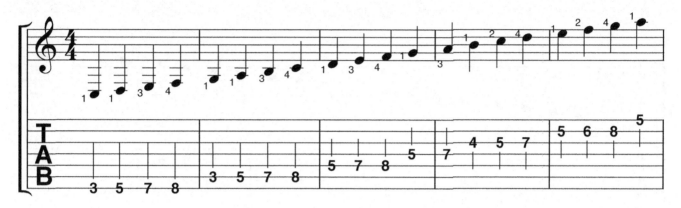

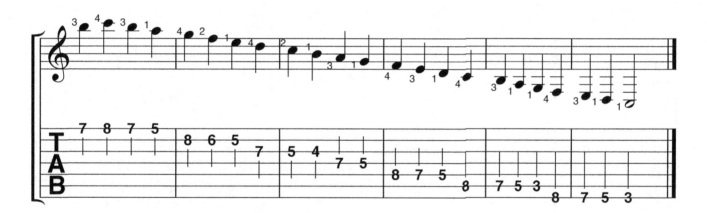

Another type of fingering is one that moves "against the grain." In other words, as the scale ascends, your hand moves down the fingerboard (from right to left). Here's an example of that type of fingering. It is illustrated here in the key of F in order to keep it in the middle of the neck.

Ex. 20
Against the grain

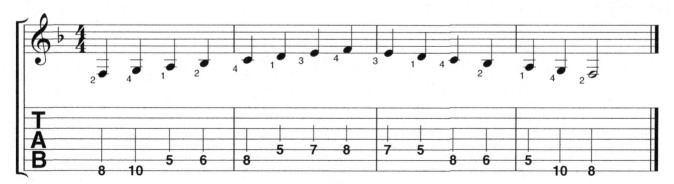

s with the horizontal fingering, this fingering can be extended up to the first string.

Ex. 21

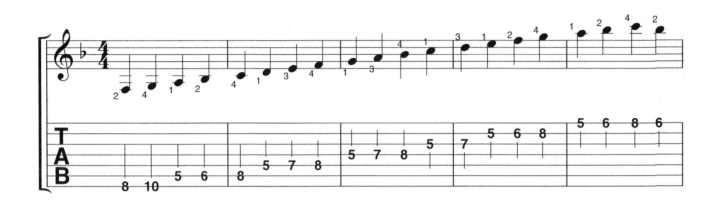

ow, a brief explanation of modes. Remember that each fingering, in addition to being a major scale, could also be given a "minor" name, a "Dorian" name, a "Mixolydian" name, etc. They are simply the same set of notes, starting at different points in the scale. For instance, if you start a C major scale on a C, you are starting on the root. If you play the exact same thing, but call it an A minor scale, the C note is now the third of the scale. If you play the exact same thing again , but this time call it a D Dorian scale, the C note is the seventh scale degree. If you play the exact same thing one more time, but call it a G Mixolydian scale, the C note is the fourth scale degree.

Y ou could continue to do this for each mode, beginning on each degree of the scale. Here is a chart that further illustrates this:

Major	Minor	Dorian	Mixolydian	etc.
Starts on root =	starts on 3rd	starts on 7th	starts on 4th	
Starts on 2nd =	starts on 4th	starts on root	starts on 5th	
Starts on 3rd =	starts on 5th	starts on 2nd	starts on 6th	
Starts on 5th =	starts on 7th	starts on 4th	starts on root	
Starts on 6th =	starts on root	starts on 5th	starts on 2nd	

W ith five fingerings, and seven modes, you could have 35 names for the same set of notes! If you don't completely understand this right now, don't worry about it. The point is, that right now, to think in terms of modes is probably not productive. It's much easier to see the fingerings as major scales and learn to apply them in that way. Shortly, we'll get to the playalong section of this chapter, and I'll illustrate again the difference between thinking in terms of major scales and modes. By the way, scales that have the same notes but different names are called "relative" to one another. C major is the relative major of A minor. A minor is the relative minor of C major. Less common, but still correct, would be to say that G Mixolydian is the relative Mixolydian of C major, and D Dorian is the relative Dorian, etc.

B e sure not to simply play the scales "up and down," but try some of the techniques described in the Introduction to Scales chapter. Get to the point where you can move around the scale freely, creating many types of melodic shapes. Concentrate on doing this at the bottom end of the scale where you are less comfortable. Finally, practice the scale with the playalong CD. Listen to how it sounds with different types of chords.

Playalong Exercise #1 (See Appendix C, No. 1)
Track 2 - Play the parallel major scale against each major 7th chord (for Cmaj7, use a C major scale).

Playalong Exercise #2 (See Appendix C, No. 1)
Track 2 - For a different sound, play the major scale a perfect fourth lower against each major 7th chord (for Cmaj7, use a G major scale). This is the same as playing in the Lydian mode.

Playalong Exercise #3 (See Appendix C, No. 2)

Track 3 - Play the major scale a whole-step lower against each minor 7th chord (for Dmi7, use a C major scale). This is the same as playing in the Dorian mode.

Playalong Exercise #4 (See Appendix C, No. 3)

Track 4 - Play the major scale a perfect fifth lower against each dominant 7th chord (for G7, use a C major scale). This is the same as playing in the Mixolydian mode.

Playalong Exercise #5 (See Appendix C, No. 4)

Track 5 - Play the major scale from the home key of all three chords in the ii-V-I chord progression (for Dmi7 - G7 - Cmaj7, use a C major scale). This is the same as playing in the Dorian mode for one bar, the Mixolydian mode for one bar, and the Ionian mode for two bars. Are you starting to see why it is easier to simply think of these as major scales?

Studies

Study No. 1 (Track 14 on CD), or play along #1 (Track 2)

This study uses the parallel major scale against each major 7th chord.

You will notice that the notes in the studies may not stay exclusively within the scale being demonstrated. This is done to make the studies sound more stylistic, and to demonstrate how the sound of the scale can be colored with some simple chromaticism without losing its fundamental character. You can hear all of the studies in section two of the CD.

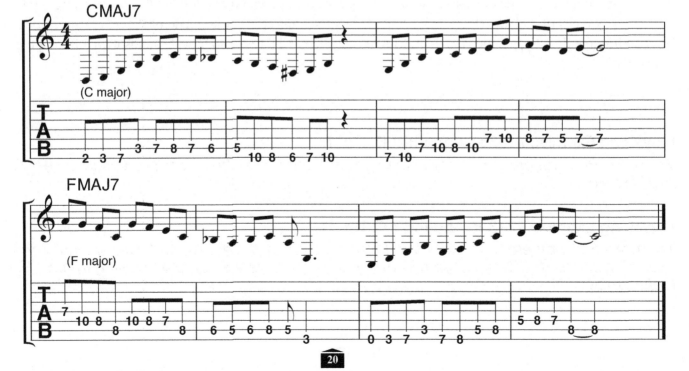

Study No. 2 (Track 15 on CD), or play along #4 (Track 5)

This study uses the major scale from the home key of all three chords in the ii-V-I chord progression.

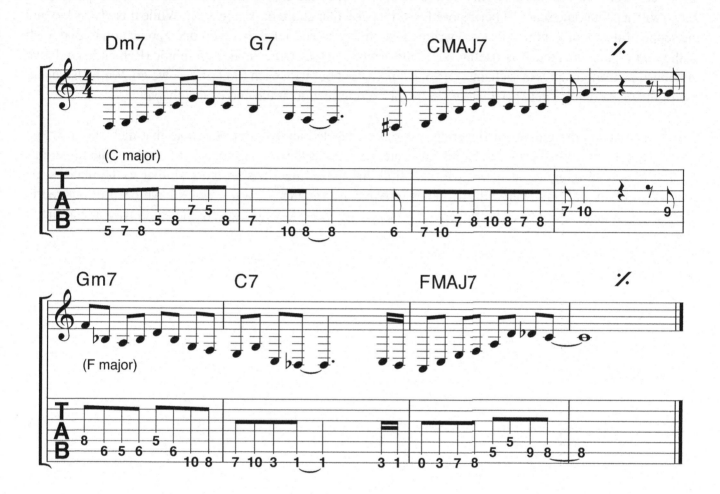

Pentatonic Scales

Pentatonic scales are simply a subset of the major scale. In other words, they are the major scale with the fourth and seventh scale degree removed. They are often used much in the same way that major scales are used, but provide a slightly different "color." They are also sometimes used in more sophisticated ways, with a pentatonic scale "superimposed" over a particular chord or progression. While this idea is beyond the scope of this book (entire books are written just on this subject), I'll give you one application to play with at the end of this chapter. It is useful to see the pentatonics as either major or minor (Remember relative relationships from the previous chapter?). So, I'll point that out with each fingering as we go. We'll also make use of the pentatonic's "dual personality" in the playalong section at the end of the chapter.

Once again, the individual fingerings have been labeled according to the note that they start on. You might notice that all of the starting notes are the same as the starting notes in the major scale fingerings (I was thinking ahead!). You will also find that these fingerings are very similar to the major scale fingerings, often the same, but with two notes missing. In some cases, a few notes have been refingered to make the scale easier to play. The fingerings transpose to other keys in exactly the same way as the major scales.

Once again, like with the major scales, the first fingering starts on the root (that is, if you want to play a **major** pentatonic). If you want to use this fingering as a minor pentatonic, then the starting note is the 3rd of the key. In other words, just like with major scales, C major pentatonic is the same as A minor pentatonic.

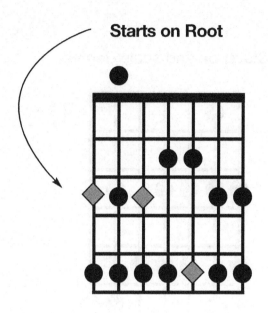

Ex. 22
Starts on root

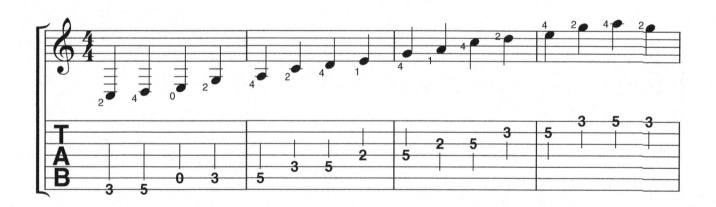

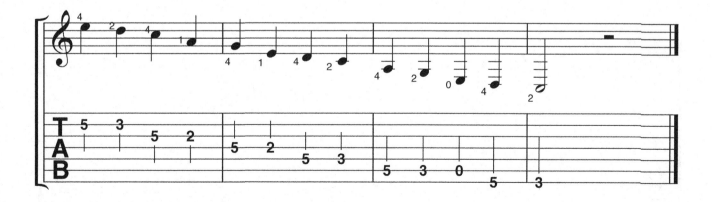

This fingering starts on the second scale degree, so to transpose it, be sure that the first note of the fingering is the second note of the scale you wish to play. In other words, to use this fingering as an F major pentatonic scale, start it on a G. To use this fingering as a B♭ major pentatonic scale, start it on a C, etc. If you want to make it a minor pentatonic, start it on the fourth scale degree. For example, to use this fingering as an F minor pentatonic, start it on a B♭.

Starts on 2nd scale degree

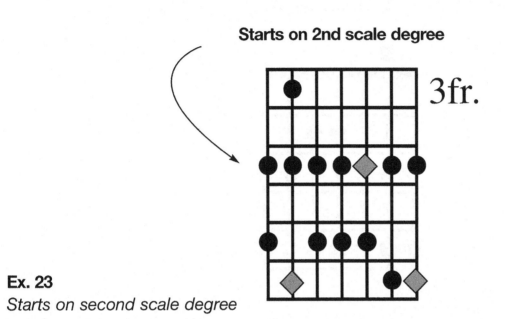

3fr.

Ex. 23
Starts on second scale degree

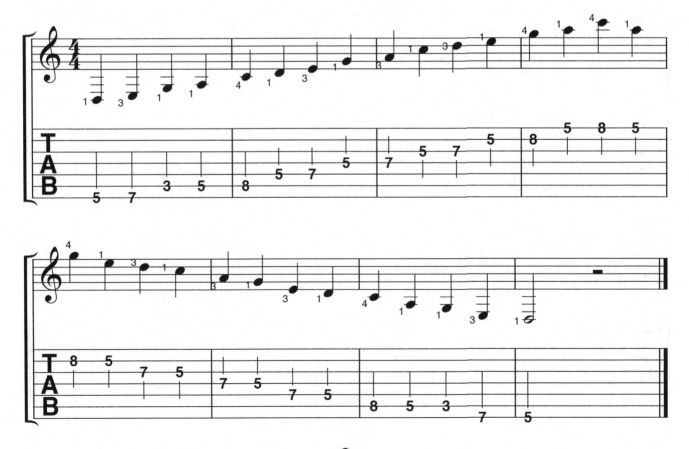

This fingering starts on the third scale degree, so to transpose it, start on the third note of the scale you wish to play. In other words, to use this fingering as an F major pentatonic scale, start it on an A. To use this fingering as a B♭ major pentatonic scale, start it on a D, etc. If you want to make it a minor pentatonic, start it on the fifth scale degree. For example, to use this fingering as an F minor pentatonic, start it on a C.

Starts on 3rd scale degree

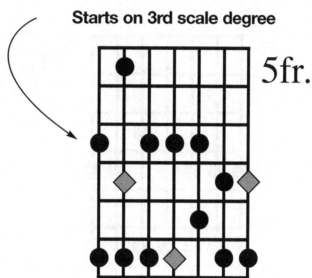

Ex. 24

Starts on third scale degree

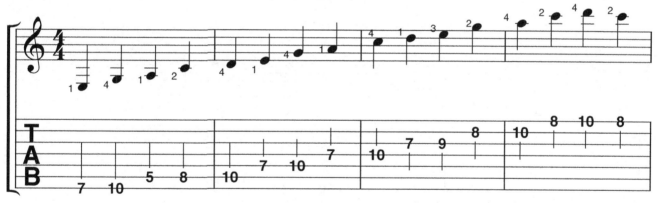

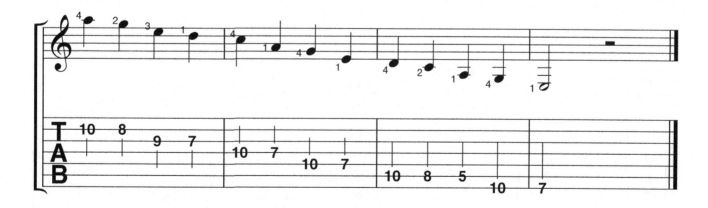

This fingering starts on the fifth scale degree, so to transpose it, start on the fifth note of the scale you wish to play. In other words, to use this fingering as an F major pentatonic scale, start it on a C. To use this fingering as a B♭ major pentatonic scale, start it on an F, etc. If you want to make it a minor pentatonic, start it on the seventh scale degree. For example, to use this fingering as an F minor pentatonic, start it on an E♭.

Starts on fifth scale degree

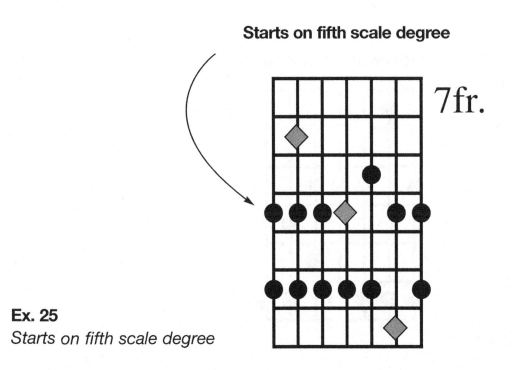

7fr.

Ex. 25

Starts on fifth scale degree

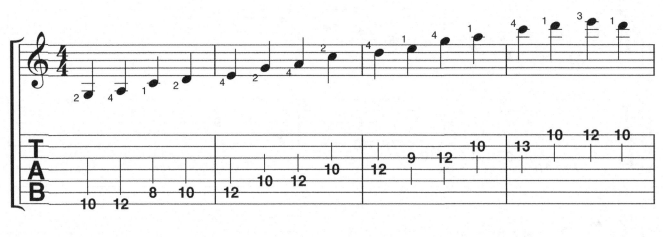

This fingering starts on the sixth scale degree, so to transpose it, start on the sixth note of the scale you wish to play. In other words, to use this fingering as an F major pentatonic scale, start it on a D. To use this fingering as a B♭ major pentatonic scale, start it on an G, etc. If you want to make it a minor pentatonic, start it on the root. For example, to use this fingering as an F minor pentatonic, simply start it on an F.

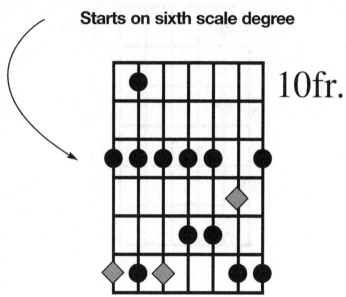

Starts on sixth scale degree

10fr.

Ex. 26
Starts on sixth scale degree

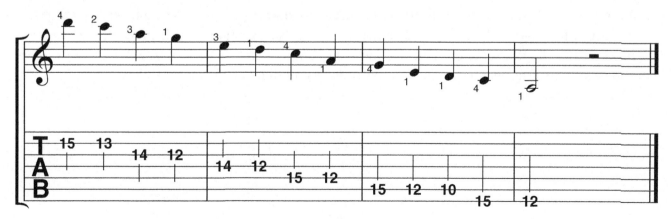

Here is a horizontal fingering for a pentatonic scale which stays on the bottom two strings. This fingering starts on the root of the major pentatonic. You could also look at it as a minor pentatonic scale starting on the third.

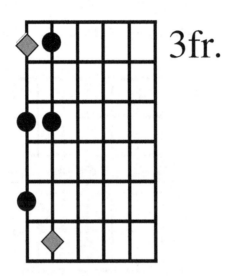

Like we did with the major scale, try to connect this horizontal fingering with one of the position fingerings to create a three octave pentatonic scale. Also experiment with playing other horizontal fingerings starting on different notes of the scale, and connect those to position fingerings as well. Finally, look for fingerings that move "against the grain" as we did with the major scales.

enerally, pentatonic scales are considered either major or minor, so there are no pentatonic modes that we need to deal with. Technically, you could call any five-note scale a pentatonic scale, since pentatonic literally means "five notes." These are usually not referred to as modes, but rather as altered pentatonics. For instance, the scale C-D-E-G-Ab might be called C pentatonic flat 6. In any event, that could be the subject of another whole book. If you know your major and minor pentatonics very well, then you could base any of the altered pentatonics off of these.

Playalong Exercise #6 (See Appendix C, No. 1)
Track 2 - Play the parallel major pentatonic scale against each major 7th chord (for Cmaj7, use a C major pentatonic scale).

Playalong Exercise #7 (See Appendix C, No. 1)
Track 2 - For a different sound, play the major pentatonic scale a perfect fourth lower against each major 7th chord (for Cmaj7, use a G major pentatonic scale). This is very similar to the last exercise, but brings out the sound of the chord's 7th instead of the root.

Playalong Exercise #8 (See Appendix C, No. 1)
Track 2 - For yet another sound, play the major pentatonic scale a major second higher against each major 7th chord (for Cmaj7, use a D major pentatonic scale). This brings out the sound of the upper extentions of the chord (7, 9, #11, and 13).

Playalong Exercise #9 (See Appendix C, No. 2)
Track 3 - Play the major pentatonic scale a whole step lower against each minor 7th chord (for Dmi7, use a C major pentatonic scale). Like we did with the major scales, we're simply playing in the home key.

Playalong Exercise #10 (See Appendix C, No. 2)
Track 3 - Play the major pentatonic scale a minor third higher against each minor 7th chord (for Dmi7, use a F major pentatonic scale). What you're really doing here is playing the parallel minor pentatonic. Remember, F major is the same as D minor.

Playalong Exercise #11 (See Appendix C, No. 4)

Track 5 - *Let's have some fun with superimposing pentatonics. Start with the major pentatonic a whole-step below the minor 7th chord, and move up in half-steps with each chord change (for Dmi7 - G7 - Cmaj7, start with a C major pentatonic, move up to a D♭ major pentatonic for the G7 chord, and move up to a D major pentatonic for the Cmaj7). These three pentatonic scales bring out the "colorful" notes of each chord. What you're actually playing on the G7 is part of an altered scale, but we're getting ahead of ourselves!*

Study No. 3 (Track 16 on CD), or play along #1 (Track 2)

This study uses the major pentatonic scale a major second higher against each major 7th chord, bringing out the sound of the upper extentions.

CMAJ7

(D major pentatonic)

FMAJ7

(G major pentatonic)

Study No. 4 (Track 17 on CD), or play along #4 (Track 5)

This study starts with the major pentatonic a whole-step below the minor 7th chord, and move up in half-steps with each chord change, bringing out the colorful notes of each chord.

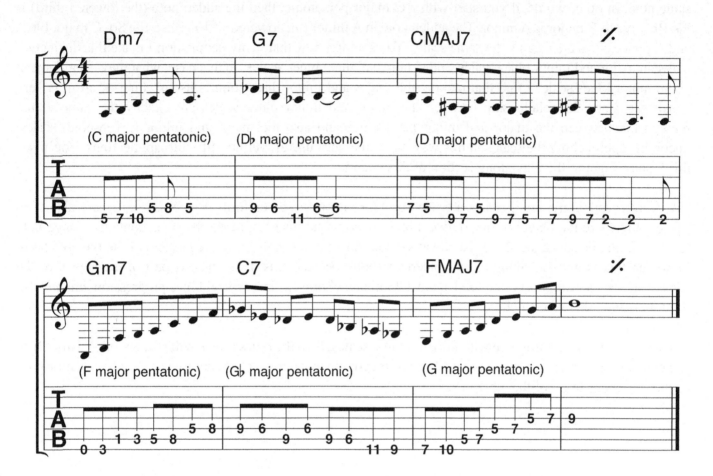

Blues Scales

A close relative of the pentatonic scale is the blues scale. A blues scale is a pentatonic scale with one extra note added. If you start with a major pentatonic scale, then the note to add is the lowered third. If you start with the minor pentatonic scale, then the note to add is the lowered fifth. Notice that if the major and minor pentatonic scales are relative to one another (the same notes), then the added note will also be the same note. In other words, if you start with a C major pentatonic, then the added note (the lowered third) is E♭. Relative to C major is A minor. The added note in A minor (the lowered fifth) is also E♭. So, C major blues and A minor blues are exactly the same scale. You should know that many people don't make this distinction between major and minor blues scales, and simply call them blues scales. In that case, what they usually mean is the minor blues scale. I find that making the major and minor distinction is useful. First of all, it is very consistent, since the relationship between the major and minor blues scales are exactly the same as the relationship between the major and minor pentatonics and also the major and minor (seven-note) scales. Secondly, approaching the scales in this way has some very useful, but not difficult, applications. You'll see this when we get to the play-along section of this chapter.

Not surprisingly, blues scales are used quite a bit on the blues form. But blues scales are also used anywhere the player wants to give a bluesy "color" to his solo. Since the scale contains a three-note chromatic sequence, there will always be dissonant notes in the scale, regardless of the type of chord. However, that is not something to be concerned about, because this dissonance is part of the appeal of the scale. Blues scales are most often used against dominant chords, as in a typical blues progression, but are also used with any other type of chord.

If you are already comfortable with the pentatonic scales, then the blues scales will come pretty easily. Once again, in some cases, a few notes have been refingered to make the scale easier to play. As always, transpose the fingerings to all of the other keys.

As usual, the first fingering starts on the root (that is, if you want to play a **major** blues scale). If you want to use this fingering as a minor blues scale, then the starting note is the 3rd of the key. In other words, just like with major and pentatonic scales, C major blues is the same as A minor blues.

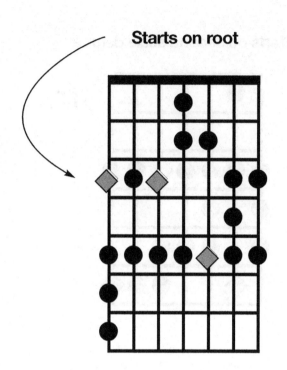

Starts on root

Ex. 28
Starts on root

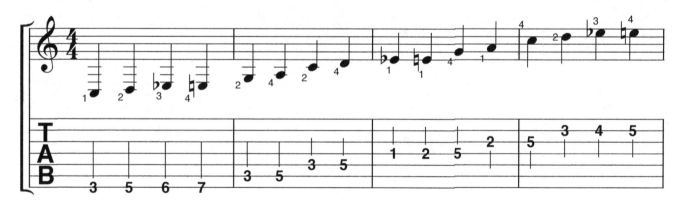

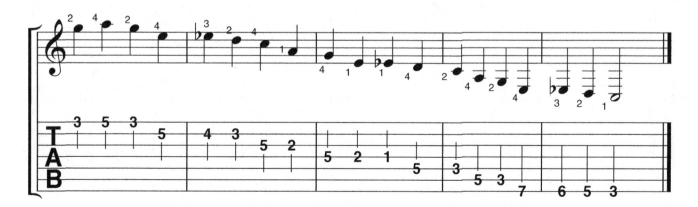

Part one - blues scales

This fingering starts on the second scale degree, so to transpose it, be sure that the first note of the fingering is the second note of the scale you wish to play. In other words, to use this fingering as an F major blues scale, start it on a G. To use this fingering as a Bb major blues scale, start it on a C, etc. If you want to make it a minor blues scale, start it on the fourth scale degree. For example, to use this fingering as an F minor blues scale, start it on a Bb.

Starts on second scale degree

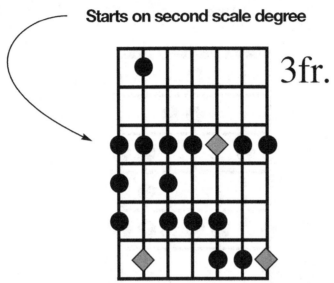

3fr.

Ex. 29

Starts on second scale degree

This fingering starts on the third scale degree, so to transpose it, start on the third note of the scale you wish to play. In other words, to use this fingering as an F major blues scale, start it on an A. To use this fingering as a B♭ major blues scale, start it on a D, etc. If you want to make it a minor blues scale, start it on the fifth scale degree. For example, to use this fingering as an F minor blues scale, start it on a C.

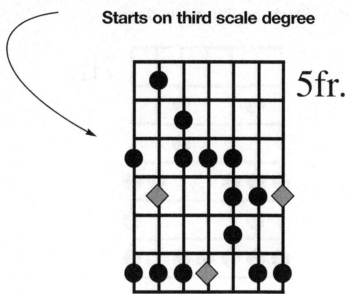

Starts on third scale degree

5fr.

Ex. 30

Starts on third scale degree

This fingering starts on the fifth scale degree, so to transpose it, start on the fifth note of the scale you wish to play. In other words, to use this fingering as an F major blues scale, start it on a C. To use this fingering as a B♭ major blues scale, start it on an F, etc. If you want to make it a minor blues scale, start it on the seventh scale degree. For example, to use this fingering as an F minor blues scale, start it on an E♭.

Starts on fifth scale degree

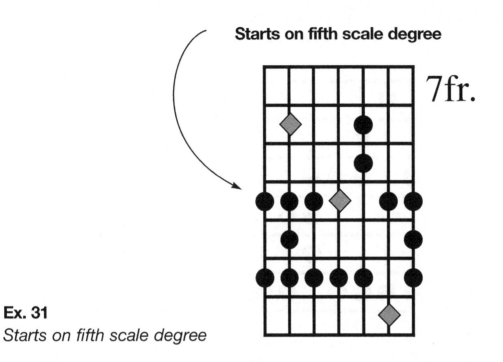

7fr.

Ex. 31

Starts on fifth scale degree

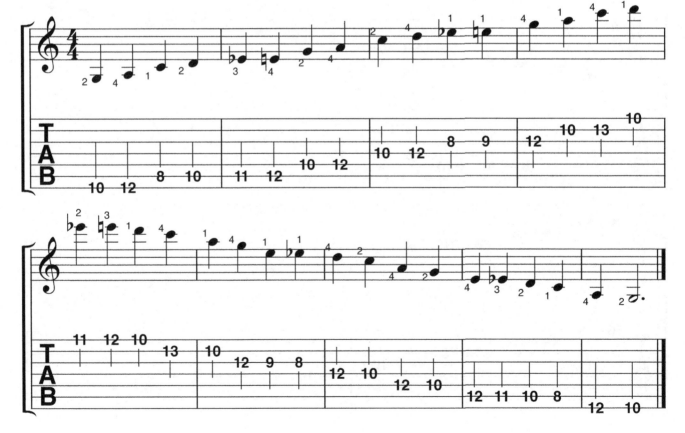

This fingering starts on the sixth scale degree, so to transpose it, start on the sixth note of the scale you wish to play. In other words, to use this fingering as an F major blues scale, start it on a D. To use this fingering as a B♭ major blues scale, start it on a G, etc. If you want to make it a minor blues, start it on the root. For example, to use this fingering as an F minor blues scale, simply start it on an F.

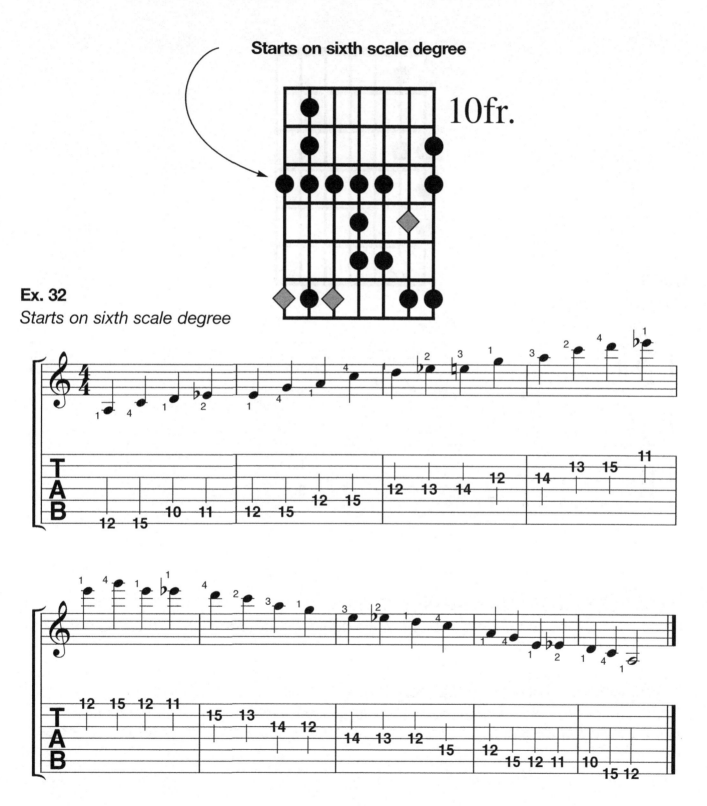

Starts on sixth scale degree

10fr.

Ex. 32

Starts on sixth scale degree

Part one - blues scales

Here is a horizontal fingering for a blues scale which stays on the bottom two strings. This fingering starts on the root of the major blues scale. You could also look at it as a minor blues scale starting on the third.

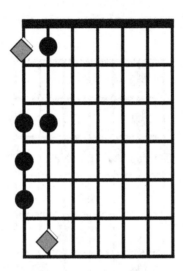

Ex. 33
Horizontal fingering

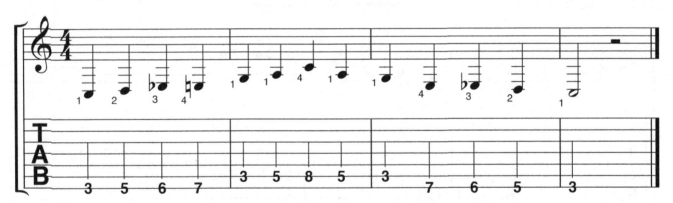

Playalong Exercise #12 (See Appendix C, No. 3)

Track 4 - Play the parallel major blues scale against each dominant 7th chord (for C7, use a C major blues scale).

Playalong Exercise #13 (See Appendix C, No. 3)

Track 4 - Play the parallel minor blues scale against each dominant 7th chord (for C7, use a C minor blues scale). Compare this sound to the sound of the previous exercise.

Playalong Exercise #14 (See Appendix C, No. 5)

Track 6 - Play a C major blues scale against the C7 chords, and play a C minor blues scale against the F7 chords.

Playalong Exercise #15 (See Appendix C, No. 6)

Track 7 - Like in the previous exercise, play a C major blues scale against the C7 chords, and play a C minor blues scale against the F7 chords. For the ii-V in bars 9 & 10, use the C major scale (not the blues scale, but the C major scale). This way you are using three different colors in a 12-bar blues.

Study No. 5 (Track 18 on CD) or play along #3 (Track 4)

This study uses a C major blues scale against the C7 chords, and a C minor blues scale against the F7 chords.

Study No. 6 (Track 19 on CD) or play along #6 (Track 7)

This study uses a C major blues scale against the C7 chords, a C minor blues scale against the F7 chords and a C major scale for the ii-V in bars 9 & 10.

Harmonic Minor Scales

While most standard tunes are in major keys, there is no shortage of tunes in minor keys as well. Also, quite frequently, tunes in major keys will temporarily slip into minor keys. As you build your repertoire of standards, it won't take you long before you run into harmonies derived from the various forms of the minor scale. Remember that natural minor scales are identical to their relative major counterparts, and as a result, don't require any new fingerings. Closely related to the natural minor is the harmonic minor, which is the same except for having a raised seventh. From a C natural minor scale, the following seventh chords can be built: Cmi7, Dmi7b5, Ebmaj7, Fmi7, Gmi7, Abmaj7 and Bb7 (notice that these are the same chords that you can get from an Eb major scale). By raising the seventh scale degree (changing the Bb to a B natural), several of the chords are changed. We now get this: Cmi(maj7), Dmi7b5, Ebmaj7(#5), Fmi7, G7, Abmaj7 and Bdim7. As you see, a couple of chords in the harmonic minor scale are sounds that you don't run into every day. On the other hand, the harmonic minor scale contains a minor ii-V, which is an extremely common and useful progression. Notice that in the natural minor scale above, that the V chord is actually minor. While this chord is sometimes used, it has more of a modal sound to it. Since virtually all standard tunes use tonal or functional harmonies, the V chord is nearly always a dominant chord. When the V chord in a minor key is made into a dominant, then this is usually harmonic minor harmony (it could also be melodic minor harmony, but we'll save that for another chapter). Also notice that the ii chord in harmonic minor is a half diminished, or a mi7b5. The most characteristic sound of harmonic minor harmony is the combination of these two chords into what is generally called a "minor ii-V." In the key of C minor, that would be Dmi7b5 to G7. If we extend the V chord one more note (out to the ninth), it becomes a G7b9. So, that same chord progression is often seen like this: Dmi7b5 to G7b9.

Familiarize yourself with the harmonic minor fingerings. Remember, they are only one note different from your major scales, but since we are using these as minor scales now, the "starting" notes are built on different scale degrees.

s usual, the first fingering starts on the root.

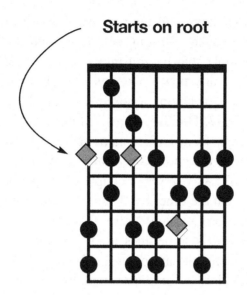

Ex. 34

Starts on root

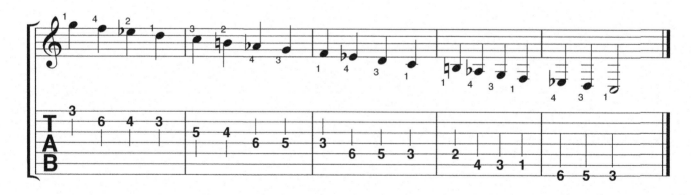

This fingering starts on the second scale degree, so to transpose it, be sure that the first note of the fingering is the second note of the scale you wish to play. In other words, to use this fingering as an F harmonic minor scale, start it on a G. To use this fingering as a B♭ harmonic minor scale, start it on a C, etc.

Starts on second scale degree

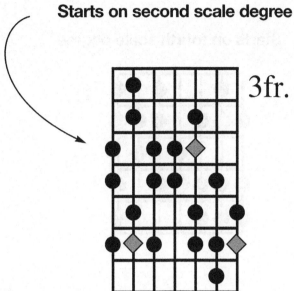

3fr.

Ex. 35

Starts on second scale degree

Part one - harmonic minor

This fingering starts on the fourth scale degree, so to transpose it, be sure that the first note of the fingering is the fourth note of the scale you wish to play. In other words, to use this fingering as an F harmonic minor scale, start it on a B♭. To use this fingering as a B♭ harmonic minor scale, start it on an E♭, etc.

Starts on fourth scale degree

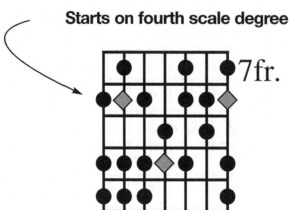

Ex. 36

Starts on fourth scale degree

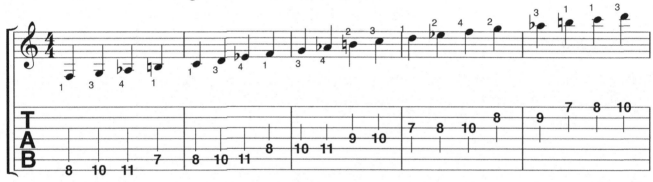

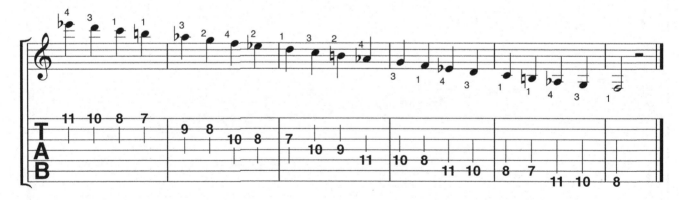

This fingering starts on the fifth scale degree, so to transpose it, be sure that the first note of the fingering is the fifth note of the scale you wish to play. In other words, to use this fingering as an F harmonic minor scale, start it on a C. To use this fingering as a B♭ harmonic minor scale, start it on an F, etc.

Starts on fifth scale degree

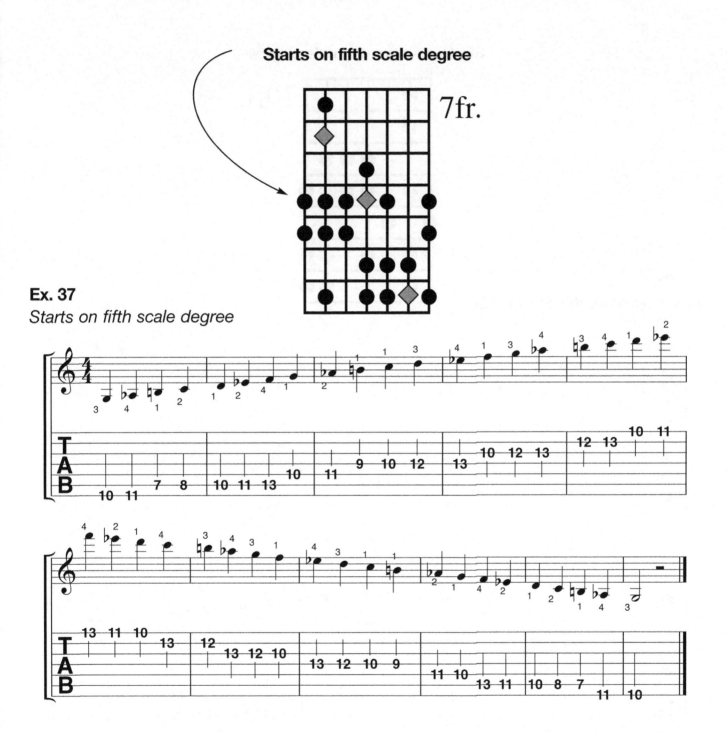

7fr.

Ex. 37

Starts on fifth scale degree

This fingering starts on the seventh scale degree, so to transpose it, be sure that the first note of the fingering is the seventh note of the scale you wish to play. In other words, to use this fingering as an F harmonic minor scale, start it on an E. To use this fingering as a B♭ harmonic minor scale, start it on an A, etc.

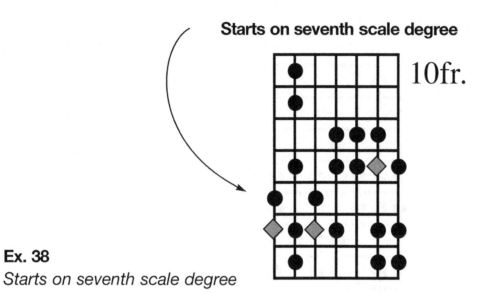

Starts on seventh scale degree

10fr.

Ex. 38

Starts on seventh scale degree

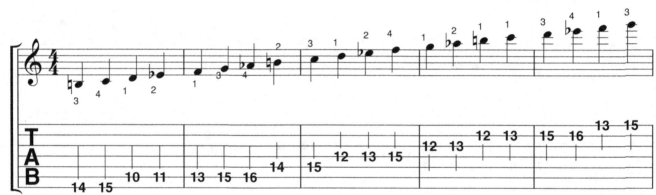

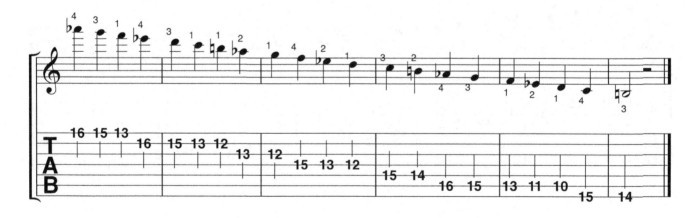

H ere is a horizontal fingering for a harmonic minor scale.

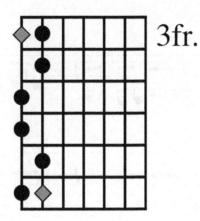

3fr.

Ex. 39

Horizontal

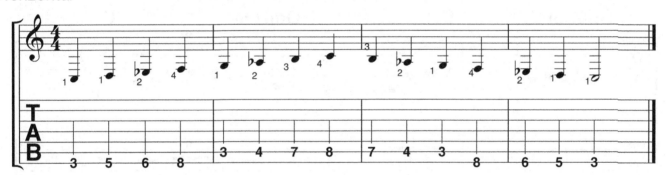

Playalong Exercise #16 (See Appendix C, No. 7)

Track 8 - Play the harmonic minor scale from the home key of the ii-V chord progression (for Dmi7♭5 - G7♭9, use a C harmonic minor scale).

Study No. 7 (Track 20 on CD) or play along #7 (Track 8)

This study uses the harmonic minor scale from the home key of the ii-V chord progression.

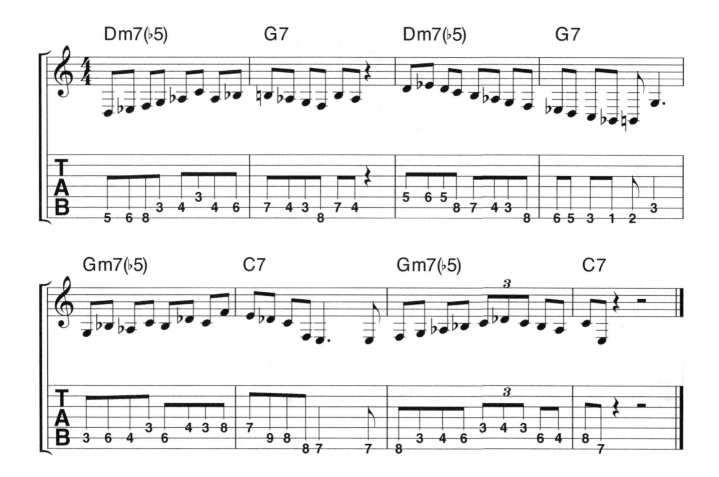

Diminished Scales

Diminished scales are often misunderstood. Both in terms of how they are constructed and how they are used. For our purposes here, let's stick to the most practical and most common fingerings and applications. First of all, about construction: diminished scales are constructed by alternating whole steps and half steps. It doesn't really matter which you start with, you will still get a diminished scale. If you start with a whole-step, you will get what is commonly referred to as a whole-step/half-step diminished scale. If you start with a half step, you will get what is commonly referred to as a half-step/whole-step diminished scale. The point is that these two scales are really the same, but starting on different notes. Further complicating (or actually simplifying) matters is that diminished scales repeat at the minor third (every third fret). In other words, a C diminished scale is exactly the same as an E♭ diminished scale, a G♭ diminished scale, and an A diminished scale. So while in theory there are 24 different diminished scales (whole-step/half-step in 12 keys, plus half-step/whole-step in 12 keys), in reality there are only three! If this is difficult for you to visualize, try working it out on paper. You can start a diminished scale on any note, and you can start with either a whole-step or a half-step, but you will only get three scales that are actually different. All the others will be the same as one of those three, but starting on a different note.

While many types of chords can be built from the notes in the diminished scale, there are only a couple of applications that are very common. The first, not surprisingly, is over a diminished chord. Generally, in this case, it is the whole-step/half-step scale that is used. Since the scale repeats at the minor third, you can build this scale from any note in the chord and you will get the same scale. Another way to look at it is that you are using the notes in the chord, plus the notes a half-step below (or a whole-step above) the notes in the chord. The other common application for diminished scales is over a dominant 7th chord. If you are building this scale from the root of the chord, then you would build a half- step/whole-step scale. You could also build a whole-step/half-step scale from the chord's 3rd, 5th, 7th, or ♭9, and you would get the same scale. If you use this scale over a dominant 7 chord, you will be coloring the chord in a very specific way.

H ere are the notes in the diminished scale that follows:

$$\boxed{\textbf{B C D E}\flat \textbf{ F G}\flat \textbf{ A}\flat \textbf{ A}}$$

T his scale is often played over an F7 chord. It is also played over an A♭7, a B7, and a D7, but let's just look at the F7 for now. First, you can see that we have the four notes of the chord (F, A, C, E♭). The other four notes are all extensions. The B is the ♯11, the D is the 13, the G♭ is the ♭9, and the A♭ is the ♯9. So, with that in mind, some chord symbols that would suggest the use of this scale would be: F13♭9, F13♯9, F7♭9♯11 and F7♯9♯11. Keep in mind that you don't have to have one of these chords to use the scale. You can play it over a plain old F7, but if you do, you'll be coloring the chord using diminished harmony. It is very important that you learn the sound of the scale, so that you can use it only when your ear tells you that it is appropriate.

L ook at the diminished scale fingerings on the following pages. The first thing you will notice is that there are only two! This is because either fingering can be repeated at the minor third (every three frets), and will be exactly the same notes.

e're going to start this time with a horizontal fingering because it's easier to play. Notice that it is simply a four-note pattern that repeats on every string.

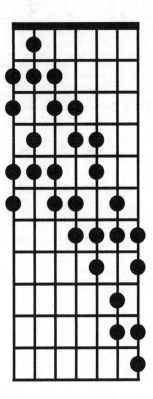

Ex. 40

The next fingering is vertical (that is, it stays in position). It starts with the same four-note pattern, but continues with a six-note pattern (starting with the sixth note of the scale) that repeats every two strings.

Ex. 41

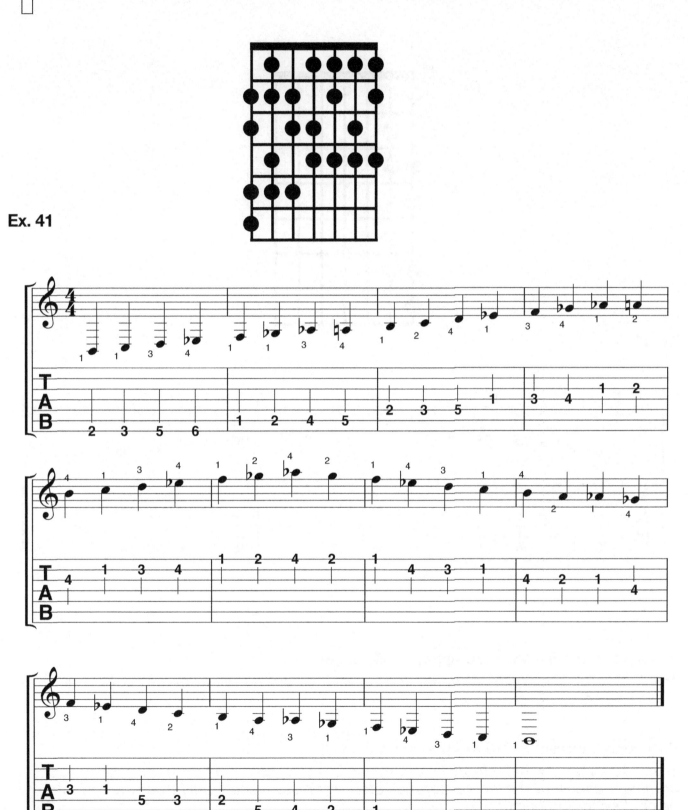

H ere's another horizontal fingering for a diminished scale, staying on the bottom two strings.

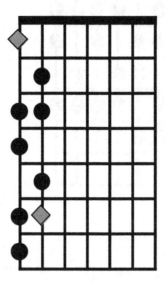

Ex. 42

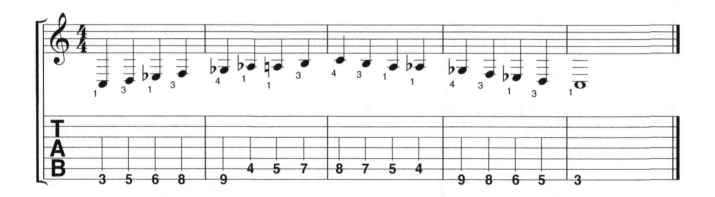

Playalong Exercise #17 (See Appendix C, No. 8)

Track 9 - *Play the whole-step/half-step diminished scale built from the root of each diminished chord.*

Playalong Exercise #18 (See Appendix C, No. 9)

Track 10 - *Play the half-step/whole-step diminished scale built from the root of each dominant chord, or the whole step/half step diminished scale built from the 3rd, 5th, 7th, or ♭9 of each dominant chord.*

Study No. 8 (Track 21 on CD) or play along #8 (Track 9)

This study uses the whole-step/half-step diminished scale built from the root of each diminished chord, and then resolves to the parallel major.

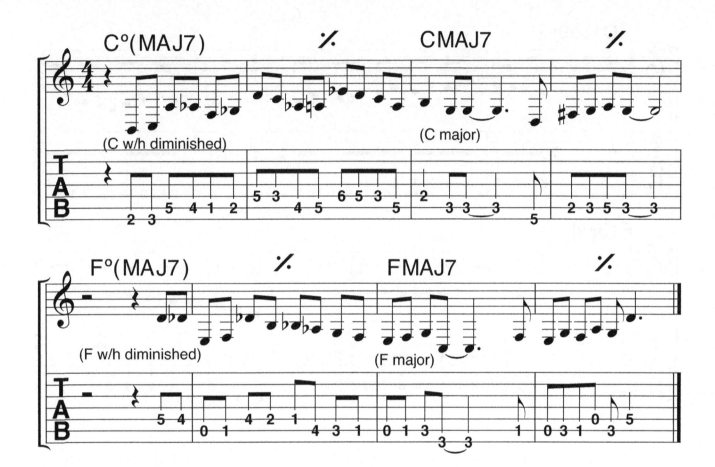

Study No. 9 (Track 22 on CD) or play along #9 (Track 10)

This study uses the half-step/whole-step diminished scale built from the root of each dominant chord.

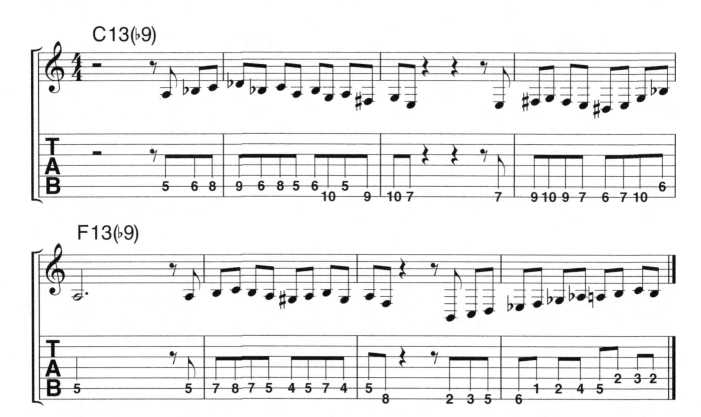

Whole – Tone Scales

Whole-tone scales, like diminished scales, repeat (or actually invert) as you move them up the fingerboard. They are constructed entirely of whole steps. Because of this, any note in a whole-tone scale can be looked at as the root. So while in theory there are 12 different whole-tone scales, in reality there are only two! Again, you can try working this out on paper to make it easier to see. If you start a whole-tone scale on C, that's one scale. Transpose it up to C♯, and that's it! There are no more. Any other whole-tone scale you can build will be the same as one of those two, but starting on a different note.

Again, like the diminished, many types of chords can be built from the notes in the whole-tone scale, but only a couple are very common. These have to do with applying this scale over a dominant 7 chord. Here are the notes in the whole-tone scale below:

> **B D♭ E♭ F G A**

This scale is often played over an F7 chord. It is also played over an a B7, a D♭7, an E♭7, a G7 and an A7, but let's just look at the F7 for now. First, you can see that we have three notes of the chord (F, A, & E♭). The other three notes are extensions or altered notes. The B is the ♭5, the D♭ is the ♯5, and the G is the 9th. So, with that in mind, some chord symbols that would suggest the use of this scale would be: F7♯5, F7♭5, F9♯5 and F9♭5. Keep in mind that you don't have to have one of these chords to use the scale. You can play it over a plain old F7, but if you do, you'll be coloring the chord using whole-tone harmony. It is very important that you learn the sound of the scale, so that you can use it only when your ear tells you that it is appropriate.

Look at the whole-tone scale fingerings on the following pages. Again, like the diminished scale, notice that there are only two fingerings. This is because either fingering can be repeated at the whole-step (every two frets), and will be exactly the same notes.

Our first fingering is horizontal (works it's way up the fingerboard). Notice that this fingering is simply a three-note pattern that repeats on every string.

Ex. 43
Horizontal whole-tone scale

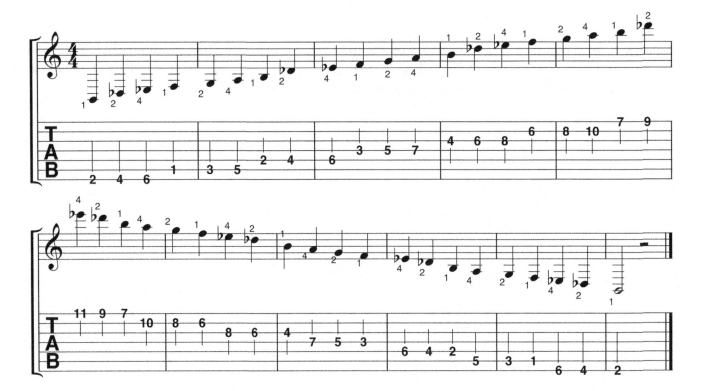

The next fingering is vertical (stays in position). Notice that this fingering also makes use of the same three-note pattern, but sometimes includes only two notes per string in order to keep the fingering in position.

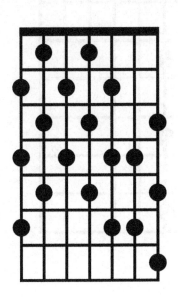

Ex. 44

Vertical whole-tone scale

Here's another horizontal fingering for a whole-tone scale, staying on the bottom two strings.

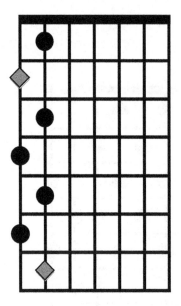

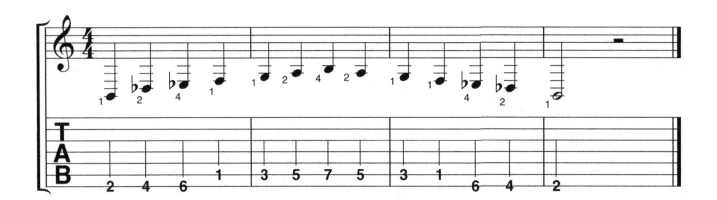

Play along Exercise #19 (See Appendix C, No. 10)

Track 11 - *Play the whole-tone scale built from the root of each dominant chord.*

Study No. 10 (Track 23 on CD) or play along #10 (Track 11)
This study uses the whole-tone scale built from the root of each dominant chord.

Melodic Minor Scales

Melodic minor scales are very colorful sounding and can be used in a variety of contexts. In traditional theory, a melodic minor scale is built by taking a natural minor scale and raising the 6th and the 7th while the scale is ascending and returning to natural minor while the scale is descending. Since we are using the scale as a tool for improvisation, it doesn't serve any purpose to play the scale in this manner. We will simply play the scale the same way (with the raised 6th and 7th), in both directions. When the scale is played like this, it is sometimes called the "jazz minor" scale. Note that with the raised 6th and 7th always in place as part of the scale, the scale is only one note different from it's parallel major scale, that note being a lowered third. From a C melodic minor scale, the following seventh chords can be built: Cmi(maj7), Dmi7, E♭maj7♯5, F7, G7, Am7♭5 and Bmi7♭5. Every mode of the melodic minor scale has an application in jazz improvisation. Some are more common than others, but each one works well given the right situation. Let's look at each scale degree.

First mode: The first mode of the melodic minor, which is of course the melodic minor itself, is often used not only over the Cmi(maj7) but also over a Cmi6. Generally when you see one of these chords, it is functioning as a tonic chord (or the i chord of the key), and so is most often found in tunes in minor keys.

Second mode: A C melodic minor scale is not used very frequently over a Dmi7 chord. However, there is another use of the second mode of melodic minor. If we change the ii chord to a D7sus, we are still within the C melodic minor scale. Now, if you use the scale to color the D7sus chord, you are actually making the chord a D13sus♭9. While the chord symbol alone is enough to give you a headache, you will probably find the sound very contemporary and interesting.

Third mode: Another very contemporary sounding chord is the III chord of the melodic minor scale. Note that you can also change this chord to an Ebmaj7♭5 and still remain within the melodic minor scale.

Fourth mode: This is perhaps the most common use of the melodic minor scale. When we play a C melodic minor scale over an F7 chord, we color the chord with a 9th, a ♯11th and a 13th. This scale is commonly referred to also as a Lydian dominant scale. Lydian because of the raised 11th, and dominant because of the lowered 7th.

Fifth mode: The V chord in melodic minor is another dominant. This time, when we play a C melodic minor scale over a G7 chord, we color the chord with a 9th, a natural 11th and a ♭13th.

Sixth mode: The sixth mode of melodic minor gives us an alternative scale for a mi7♭5 chord. If you recall, mi7♭5 was also the vii chord in a major scale. So, over an Ami7♭5, you could play a B♭ major scale (this is the locrian mode), or you could play a C melodic minor scale. These two scales turn out to be only one note different. The B♭ major scale contains a "B♭", and the C melodic minor scale contains a "B." The note "B♭" is very dissonant against an Ami7♭5, so using the C melodic minor scale instead takes away a dissonance and instead adds a very colorful note (a 9th). When used in this context, the scale is often called a locrian ♮2 scale.

Seventh mode: The vii chord of melodic minor turns out to be another mi7♭5 chord, but this is generally not how this mode is used. We can change the Bmi7♭5 chord to an altered B7 chord and still remain within the C melodic minor scale. This is another very common use of the melodic minor scale and brings the total number of dominant chords derived from any melodic minor scale to three. If we look at the C melodic minor scale in terms of the B7 chord, we get the following notes:

C	D	E♭	F	G	A	B
▾	▾	▾	▾	▾	▾	▾
♭9	♯9	3rd	♭5	♯5	7th	root

Notice that both the 5th and the 9th are both raised and lowered. From these notes, you can build any of these altered B7 chords:

B7♭5♭9	B7♭5♯9	B7♯5♭9	B7♯5♯9

When we use the seventh mode of the melodic minor scale over any of these altered chords, it is generally referred to as an altered scale. Now there's a scale name that's easy to remember!

Part one - melodic minor

Familiarize yourself with the melodic minor fingerings. Remember, they are only one note different from your major scales.

Starts on root

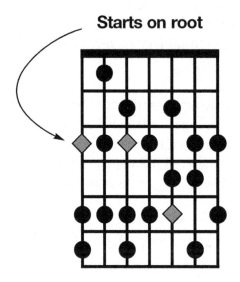

Ex. 46

Starts on root

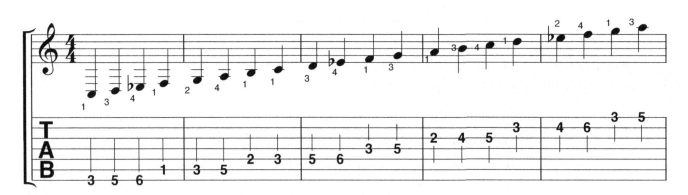

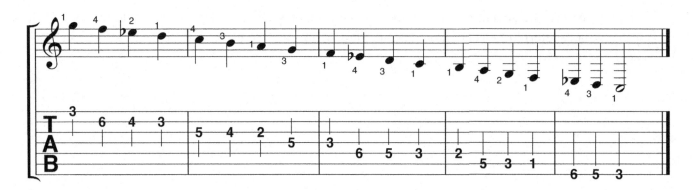

Starts on second scale degree

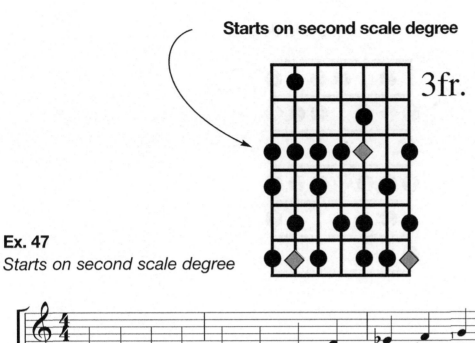

3fr.

Ex. 47

Starts on second scale degree

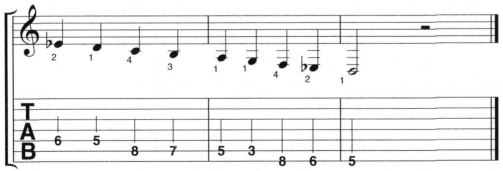

Starts on fourth scale degree

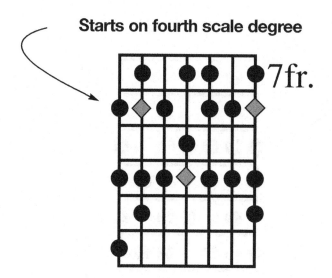

7fr.

Ex. 48
Starts on fourth scale degree

Starts on fifth scale degree

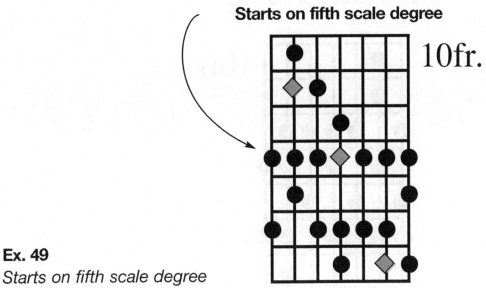

10fr.

Ex. 49

Starts on fifth scale degree

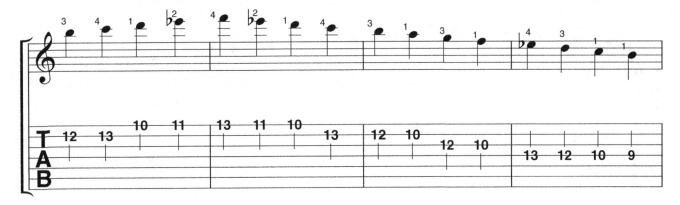

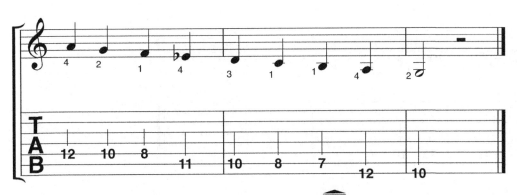

Starts on sixth scale degree

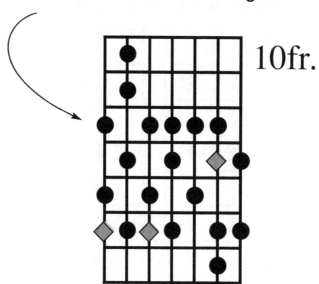

Ex. 50

Starts on sixth scale degree

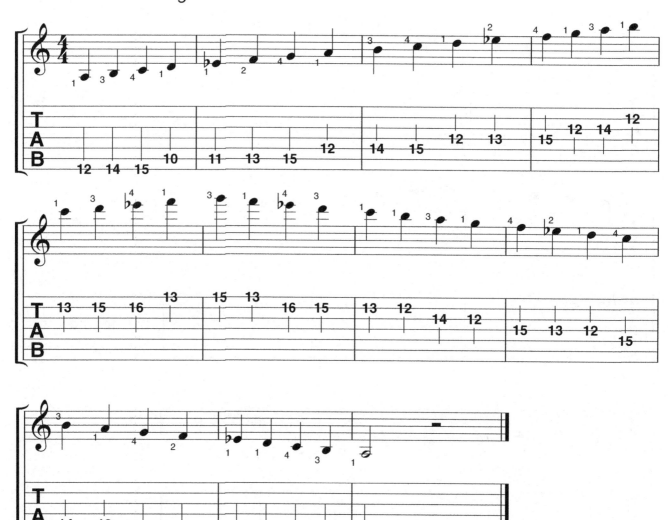

In addition to the position fingerings, below you will find two horizontal fingerings which you might find useful for melodic minor and all of it's modes. Notice that the seventh mode of the melodic minor scale starts like a diminished scale (half-step/whole-step) and the second half of the scale is built like a whole-tone scale. In fact, sometimes the scale is called a diminished whole-tone scale (but I wouldn't recommend that you call it that). Because of this, you can combine the fingering patterns we used for the diminished and whole-tone scales into melodic minor fingerings.

This first one begins with the diminished pattern and alternates with the whole-tone pattern. It is still a C melodic minor scale (or a B altered scale starting on the root).

Ex. 51
Fretboard diagram

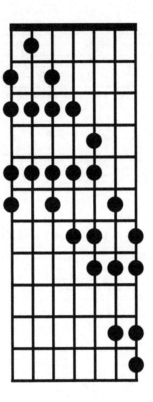

Ex. 51
Notes and tabulature

This fingering uses the same two patterns, but starts with the whole-tone pattern and alternates with the diminished pattern. It has been transposed to an F♯ melodic minor scale (or a B Lydian dominant scale starting on the root).

Ex. 52

Fretboard diagram

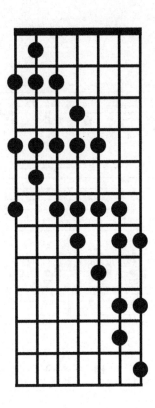

Ex. 52

Notes and tabulature

Here's another horizontal fingering for a melodic minor scale, staying on the bottom two strings.

Ex. 53
Melodic minor horizontal

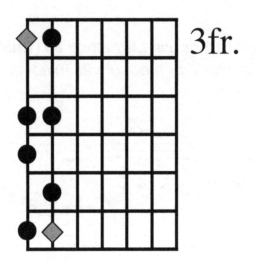

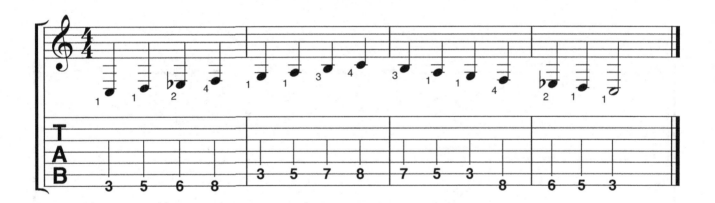

Playalong Exercise #20 (See Appendix C, No. 3)

Track 4 - Play the fourth mode of the melodic minor scale for each dominant chord (for G7, use a D melodic minor scale).

Playalong Exercise #21 (See Appendix C, No. 11)

Track 12 - Play the seventh mode of the melodic minor scale for each altered dominant chord (for G7, use an A♭ melodic minor scale).

Playalong Exercise #22 (See Appendix C, No. 12)

Track 13 - *Let's finish this section with a challenging exercise. For each ii-V-i progression, we can use three different melodic minor scales. Over the ii chord, play the sixth mode of melodic minor (for Dmi7♭5, play F melodic minor). Over the altered V chord, play the seventh mode of melodic minor (for G7alt, play A♭ melodic minor). And over the i chord, play the first mode of melodic minor (for Cmi(maj7) or Cmi6, play C melodic minor).*

Study No. 11 (Track 24 on CD) or use play along #3 (Track 4)

This study uses the fourth mode of the melodic minor scale for each dominant chord.

Study No. 12 (Track 25 on CD) or play along #11 (Track 12)

This study uses the seventh mode of the melodic minor scale for each altered dominant chord.

Study No. 13 (Track 26 on CD) or play along #12 (Track 13)

This study uses the sixth mode of melodic minor over the ii chords, the seventh mode of melodic minor over the altered V chords, and the first mode of melodic minor over the i chords.

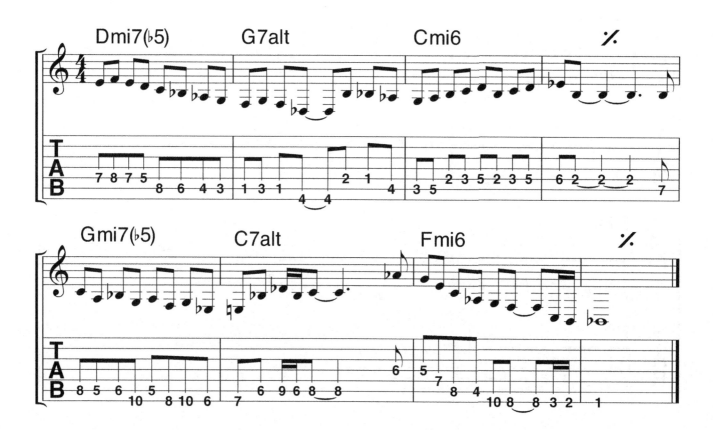

Part Two

Arpeggios

Like scales, arpeggios have been used by musicians for centuries to build technique on their instruments. Again, like with scales, this would be reason enough to learn your arpeggios. But to the improviser, there are many other reasons to learn arpeggios as well. It is not very often that you will want to insert a two- or three-octave arpeggio in the middle of a jazz solo. However, learning arpeggios will help you visualize where on the neck the chord tones lie. That's important for several reasons. First of all, you might want to emphasize the chord tones in your solo, (particularly on a traditional or swing style tune). You also might want to "target" the chord tones using various chromatic approach techniques and rotations, as is often done in a bebop style. In a more modern composition, you may want to superimpose one chord over another in order to bring out the upper extensions of the chord. Finally, you need to know where the chord tones fall on the guitar, even if your goal is to avoid them all together!

In this section, we will start with the most fundamental of all arpeggios, major and minor triads. Then we'll move on to the basic seventh chords and symmetrical chord types. With each new chord type, there is a study that focuses first on the bottom two strings, and then demonstrates how to connect the low A string with the upper six. Each study starts the arpeggio on each chord tone, so as to cover the entire neck. As with the scale fingerings in the previous section, keep in mind that they are only suggestions, and you may alter them as you wish. The last part of this section will cover a couple of different approaches to extended chords.

Be sure to transpose these studies to other keys. Since all of these studies start on the root of the chord, that shouldn't present too much of a problem. Change octaves as needed at the beginning of a new phrase.

Part two - arpeggios

This first study uses a C major triad. You start on each chord tone with a one-octave arpeggio on the bottom two strings. Following that, the arpeggio is extended for three octaves, integrating the bottom two strings with the remaining five. Once you get this study under your fingers, you could try playing major arpeggios along with the play-along CD. Use play along 1, and play four bars of the C major arpeggio (any position or fingering you like). Then do the same thing for F major, B♭ major, etc.

Ex. 54

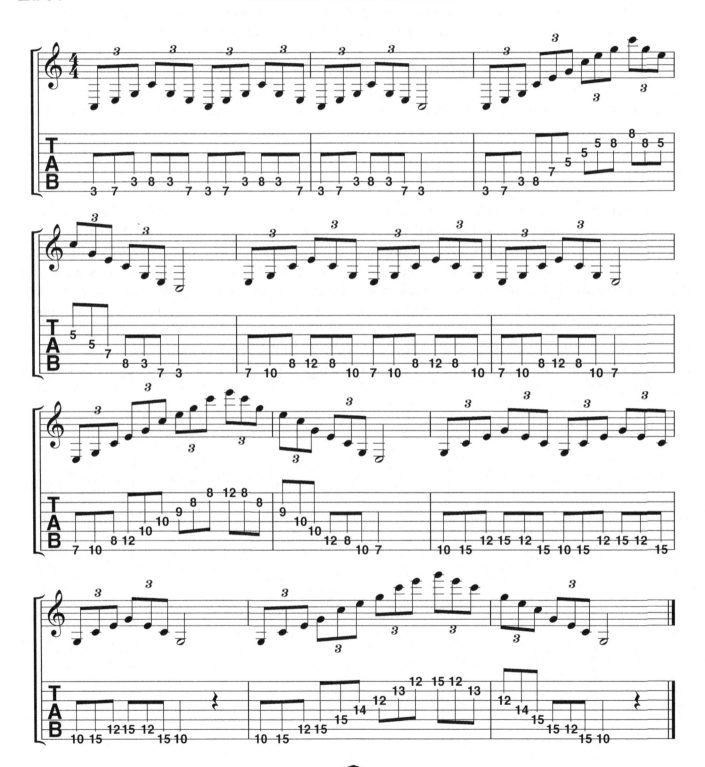

Major Triad Arpeggios

Here's a similar study using a C minor arpeggio. Again, you can also try playing minor triads with the play-along CD. Use play along 2 and play minor triads in any configuration you like for four bars each.

Minor Triad Arpeggios

Ex. 55

N ow it's time to add sevenths to our chords. We'll start with a major seventh chord. Again, the study starts the arpeggio on each chord tone, works the bottom two strings first, then extends the arpeggio through three octaves. Notice that the seventh chords cover a little more distance than the triad arpeggios did. To practice these with the play-along CD, use play along 1.

Ex. 56

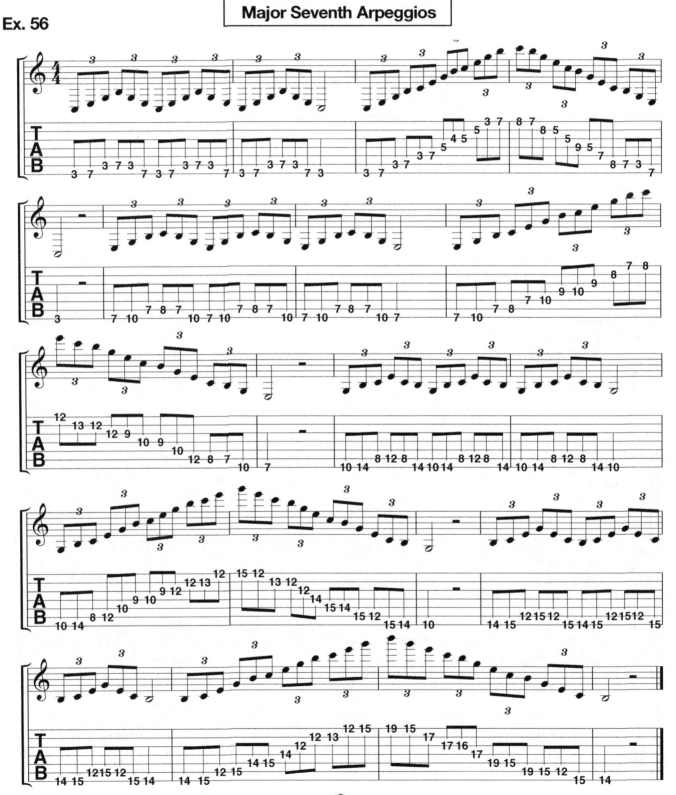

Major Seventh Arpeggios

Here's a study using dominant seventh chords. To practice these with the play-along CD, use play along 3.

Dominant Seventh Arpeggios

Ex. 57

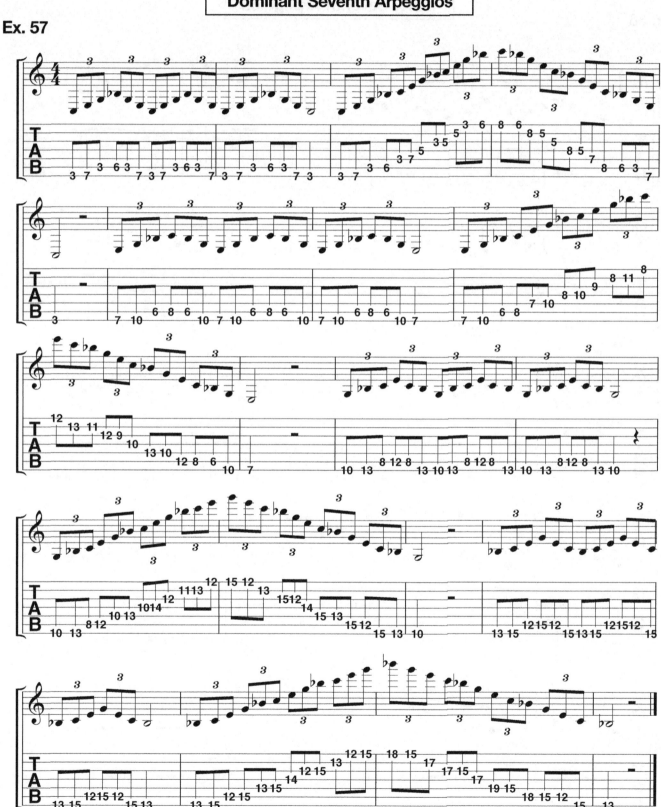

ere's a study using minor seventh chords. To practice these with the play-along CD, use play along 2. For more of a challenge, use play along 4 and change from minor seventh, to dominant seventh, to major seventh, at the appropriate time.

Minor Seventh Arpeggios

Ex. 58

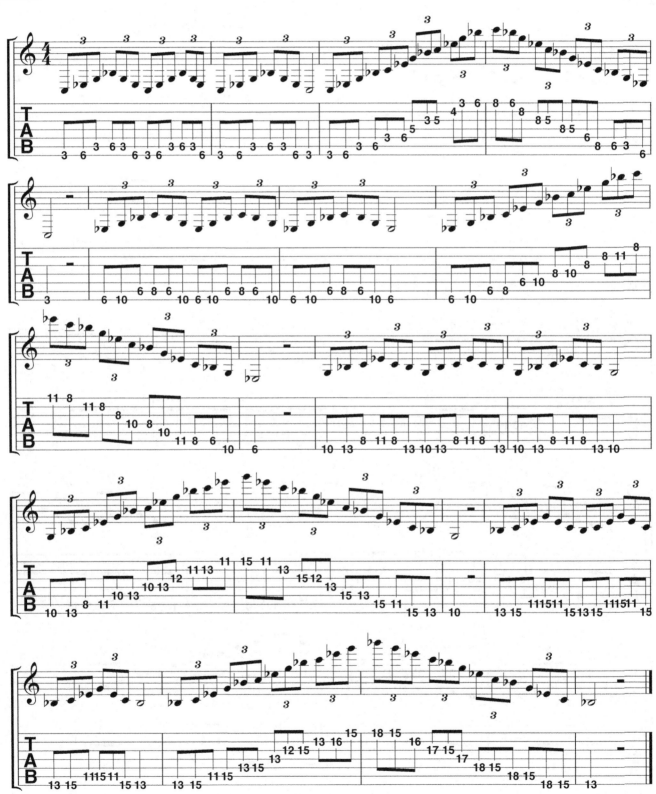

ere's a study using minor seventh ♭5 chords. To practice these with the play-along CD, use play along 7, and change from the minor seventh ♭5 arpeggio to the dominant seventh arpeggio at the appropriate time.

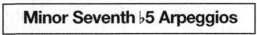

Ex. 59

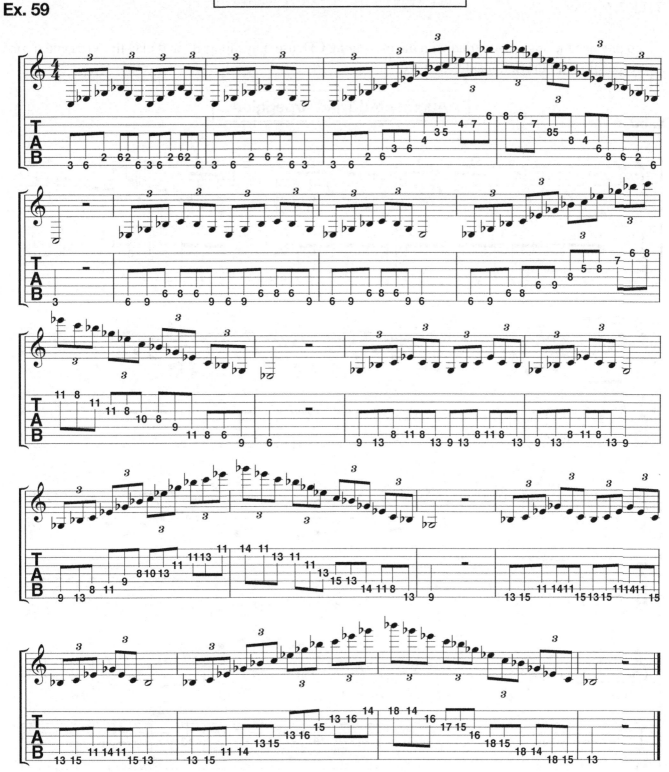

Part two - arpeggios

The next two studies cover a couple of commonly used symmetrical chords. These are chords that are built by stacking the same interval. The augmented triad is built by stacking major thirds, and the diminished seventh chord is built by stacking minor thirds. You will see that as you move these arpeggios up the neck, the fingering doesn't change. You simply move the entire structure up four frets in the case of the augmented triad, and three frets in the case of the diminished seventh chord. It is also handy to note that any note in the chord may be considered the root. In other words, the chord C-Eb-Gb-A could be called C°7, Eb°7, Gb°7 or A°7.

To practice the augmented triad with the play-along CD, use play along 10, and play the augmented triad arpeggio with the dominant 9♯5 chord.

Augmented Triad Arpeggios

Ex. 60

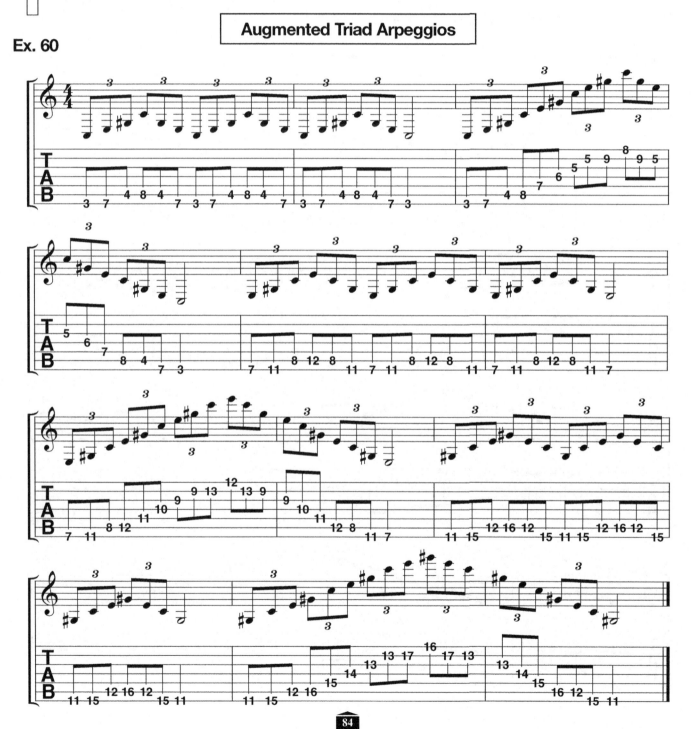

To practice the diminished seventh arpeggio with the play-along CD, use play along 8, and play the diminished arpeggio for two bars, and then resolve it to a major seventh arpeggio.

Ex. 61

Diminished Seventh Arpeggios

There are many more arpeggios for three and four-note chords on which you might want to work. Learn the basic ones very well first. Then the others can be approached as modifications to those. Some of the more useful ones would include: sus triads, dominant seventh ♭5 chords, dominant seventh ♯5 chords, and minor/major seventh chords. Note that major sixth chords are the same as their relative minor seventh chords (C6 is the same as Ami7). Also, minor sixth chords are the same as their relative minor seventh ♭5 chords (Cmi6 is the same as Ami7♭5).

Extended Arpeggios

Now that you have a handle on some basic arpeggios, we can start to extend the arpeggios by adding 9ths, 11ths, and 13ths. One way to do this is to start with the basic (seventh chord) arpeggio, and then to continue up the chord adding the extentions. These will all be presented in the key of F in order to keep them in the middle of the neck. You should, as usual, practice moving them to other keys. This first one is an F (Maj.13) arpeggio (that is, all of the notes are diatonic to an F major scale).

Ex. 62

Fmaj13

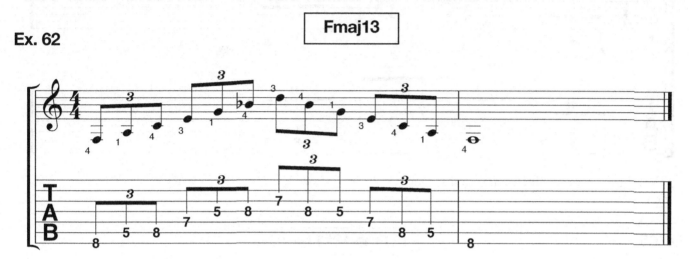

Here's another fingering for the same arpeggio, this time starting on the first finger.

Ex. 63

Fmaj13

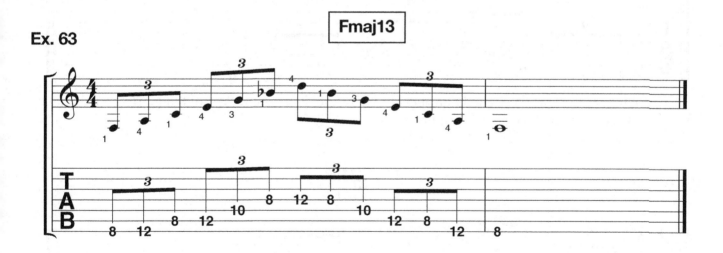

You could also start this same arpeggio on your second finger, but except for the first note, the rest of the fingering would be the same as the one given in example 63. Likewise, if you start on your third finger, the rest of the fingering would be the same as example 62. So, the most comfortable fingerings for this type of arpeggio are those that start on the first or fourth fingers, so we'll focus on those.

In a major chord, the diatonic 11th is a very dissonant note, so it's not uncommon to raise that note changing the chord to a maj13#11. Here's a fingering for that arpeggio, starting again on the fourth finger.

Ex. 64   Fmaj13#11

And here it is starting on the first finger.

Ex. 65   Fmaj13#11

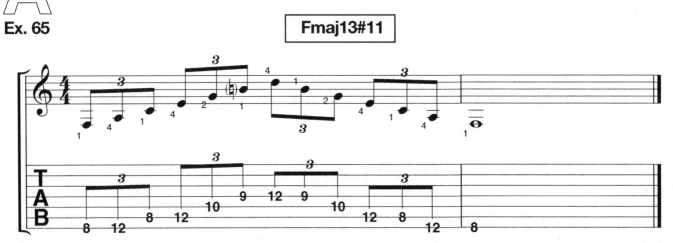

Moving from major chords to dominant chords, we can do the same type of thing. Here's a dominant 13 chord, starting with the fourth finger.

Ex. 66   F13

And here it is, starting on the first finger.

Ex. 67

Like with maj13 chords, often the 11th is raised. Here are both fingerings for this chord.

Ex. 68

Ex. 69

Moving now from dominant chords to minor chords, here are a couple of fingerings for a minor 13th (mi13) chord.

Ex. 70   Fmi13

Ex. 71   Fmi13

Often in a minor chord, and particularly when the chord is a tonic minor, the seventh is raised. Here are the fingerings for a minor 13 chord with a major 7th.

Ex. 72   Fmi13(maj7)

Ex. 73

Fmi13(maj7)

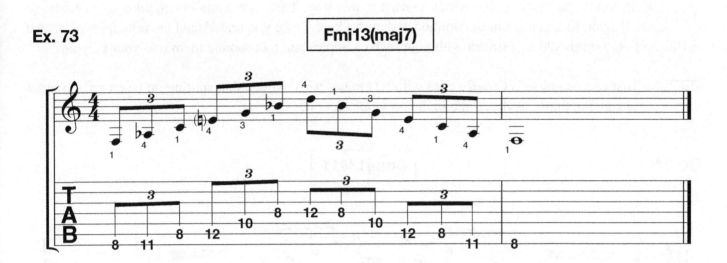

There are many other types of 13th chords, but these are the most common and useful. By all means, experiment with other types. Anything that you practice that crosses from the seventh string to the others will make you more comfortable with the low A string and allow you to incorporate it into your everyday playing.

Polychord Arpeggios

Another way to extend your arpeggios is to stack one basic chord on top of another to form a polychord. Both triads and seventh chords can be used in this way. There are countless chord combinations, so we'll again focus on the most common and useful here. Once you understand the principles presented in this section, you should experiment with your own examples and incorporate them into your playing.

This first one combines a Cmaj7 chord with a D major triad. Notice that starting on beat two, the notes are stacked in thirds, as they were in the previous section.

Ex. 74

Cmaj13#11

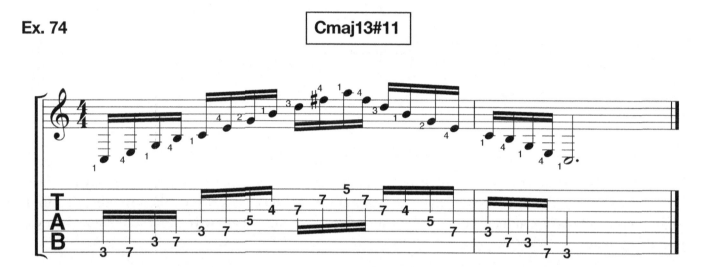

This next one combines the same two chords, but in a different configuration. Here, we start with stacked thirds, but once we reach the 13th, we continue up the D triad until we reach the top of the arpeggio.

Ex. 75

Cmaj13#11

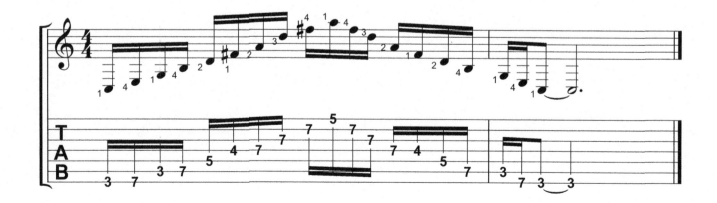

Continuing with the Cmaj7/D combination, this next one is like the last except that the Cmaj7 chord is inverted. That is, it begins on the chord third. You could also start on the chord's fifth, or the chord's seventh. You can see that inverting one, and/or the other chord of the pair would generate many variations on this idea.

Ex. 76

Cmaj13#11

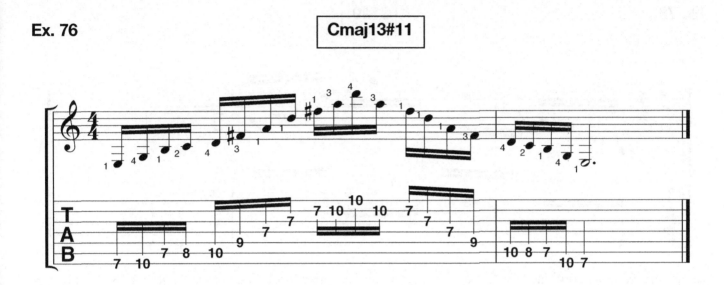

In this next one, the Cmaj7 chord is replaced with an open C major triad. This open triad shape lays very nicely on the seven-string guitar, which makes it ideal to combine with other chords to produce some interesting sounds. Notice that since the chord seventh has been omitted from the C chord, this combination may be used with either a major or a dominant type chord.

Ex. 77

Cmaj13#11 or C13#11

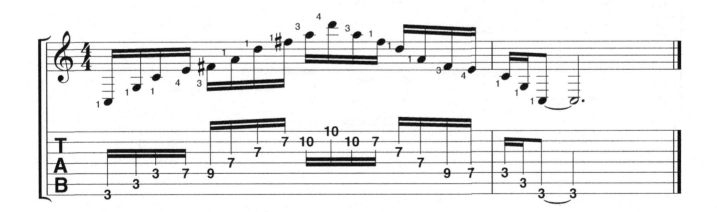

The next two examples use the open C major triad, but with different triads stacked on top. This first one combines the C major triad with an E♭ major triad. The E♭ triad adds the note B♭, which gives the chord a dominant sound. It also adds the note E♭, which is the ♯9 of the C chord. The note G is common to both chords.

Ex. 78   C7#9

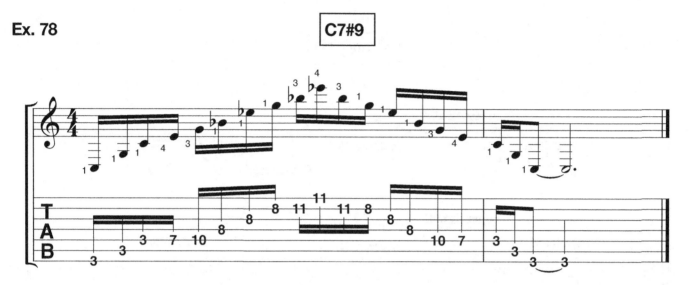

This example combines the C major triad with an G♭ major triad. The Gb triad again adds the note B♭, which gives the chord a dominant sound. It also adds the note D♭, which is the ♭9 of the C chord and the note G♭ which is the ♭5 or ♯11 of the C chord. This chord combination can be used effectively with any altered C7 chord.

Ex. 79   C7♭9♯11 or C7alt.

The next two examples combine an open C minor triad with other triads. This first one combines the C minor triad with a D minor triad to form a Cmi13 arpeggio.

Ex. 80   Cmi13

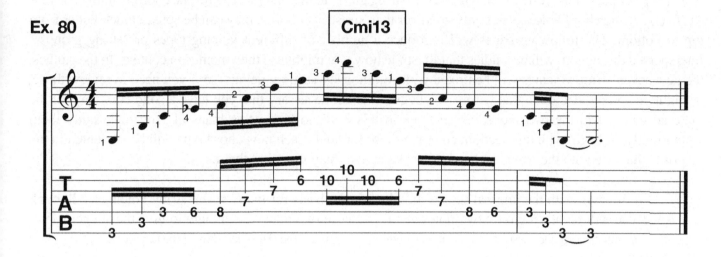

This next one combines the C minor triad with a G major triad to form a Cmi9(maj7) arpeggio.

Ex. 81   Cmi9(maj7)

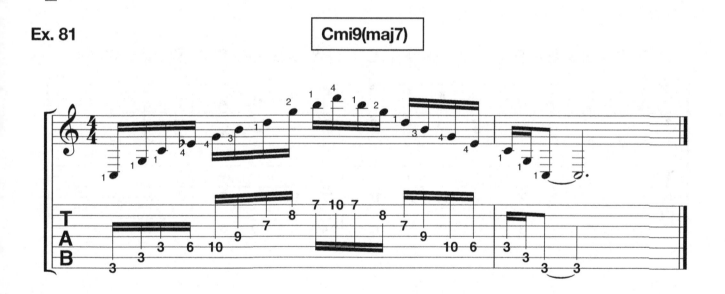

As you can see by now, by using different triad and seventh chord pairs, switching chords in different registers, inverting chords and using different types of voicings, we can generate countless variations using the polychord idea. Once again, experiment, have fun, and find the ones that best suit your style of playing.

Part Three - Chord Voicings I

While the previous two sections of this book focused on melodic uses of the 7th string, the reason most people get interested in playing seven-string guitar in the first place is for the chord voicings. Seven-string chord voicings not only go lower than six-string chords, they can be spread much wider from top to bottom. The following pages will introduce a number of different voicing types or "string groups." Interspersed throughout will be studies that illustrate how you might use the voicings in context. In the studies, the new seven-string voicings will be mixed with common six-string voicings, so if you need to review those, it might be a good idea to do that before you begin. It is not necessary that you have a solid command of the material covered in the two preceding sections in this book to begin this material. You may study them concurrently, or begin with this section, and save those for later. Each new chord type will be presented in the key of C, but like with the scales and arpeggios, be sure to play them in other keys.

We'll begin with the interval of a 10th, which is the basis for many seven-string voicings. Although you will be playing only two notes at a time, these two notes are enough to give the suggestion of a larger chord and these voicings are very effective. Here are the diatonic 10ths in the key of C.

Ex. 82

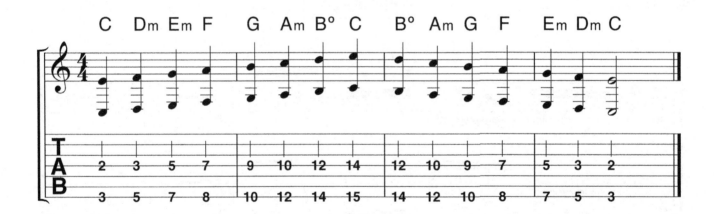

Most of the time you will use the 10ths with notes added, or in conjunction with other types of voicings. Occasionally, you may want to use them by themselves, usually to make a "walking" type of accompaniment. Study number 14 is a 12-bar blues that makes extensive use of 10th intervals.

Study No. 14 (Track 27 on CD)

M any seven-string voicings can be generated by adding notes to these tenth intervals. The first note we'll add is the chord's 7th. Here are the basic 10th voicings with the chord seventh added above on the third string. You may have already played these as six- string voicings with the bass notes raised an octave.

Ex. 83

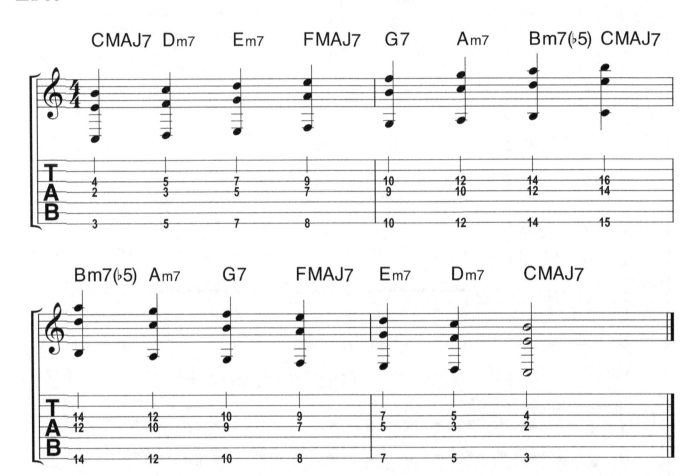

S tudy no. 15 combines these new three-note voicings with some six-string voicings that you probably already know. It illustrates how you could use these voicings to play in a "Freddie Green" style of rhythm guitar playing.

Study No. 15 (Track 28 on CD)

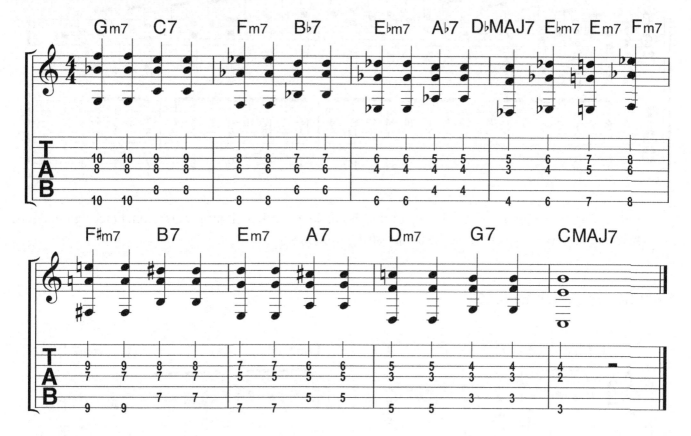

T he seventh may also be replaced with a 6th. Notice that in some cases, rather than forming a sixth chord, this creates an inversion of a triad. If you're not familiar with inversions, see **Appendix A: An Explanation of Inversions.**

Ex. 84

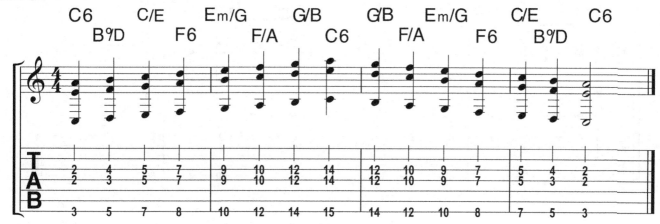

You can even move the 7th to the 6th and create a moving voice on top of the chords.

Ex. 85

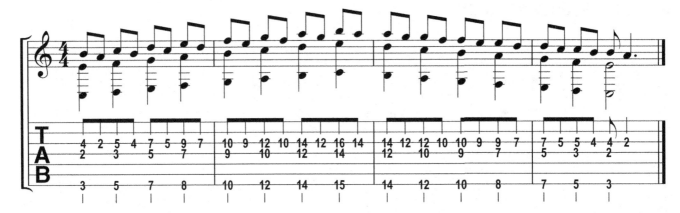

Study no. 16 uses moving voices on top of the chords in a familiar chord progression. Once again, notice how the new voicings are mixed with six-string voicings.

Study No. 16 (Track 29 on CD)

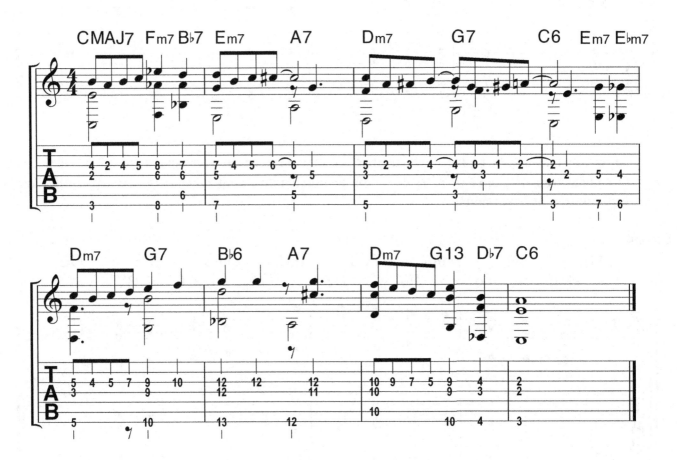

Next, add the 5th to the voicings in example 83 on the sixth string. This forms what is known as a "drop-2 and -4" voicing. If you're not familiar with this terminology, see **Appendix B: An Explanation of Voicing Types.**

Ex. 86

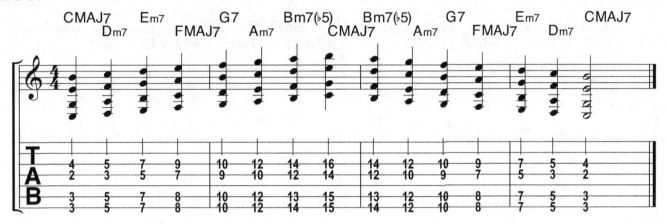

These voicings are spread rather wide and would rarely be used in comping. They are, however, effective in a solo context, as shown in study no. 17.

Study No. 17 (Track 30 on CD)

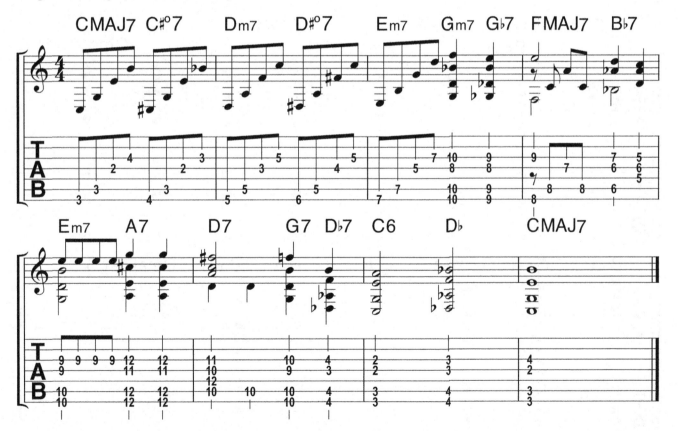

The chord's 5th may also be added above that same voicing, on the first string.

Ex. 87

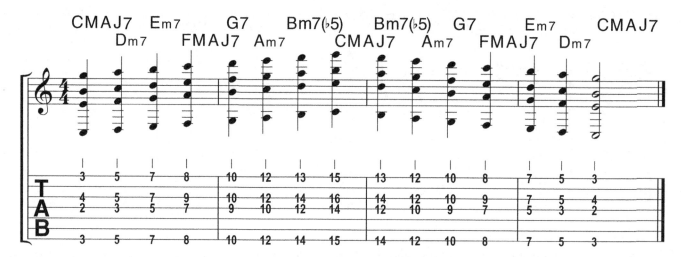

The 5th may be replaced with the 11th. Notice that in the example below, not all of the 11ths are diatonic. It's unusual to add a natural 11th to a major or dominant chord, so you will probably find it more useful to raise the 11th on those chord types.

Ex. 88

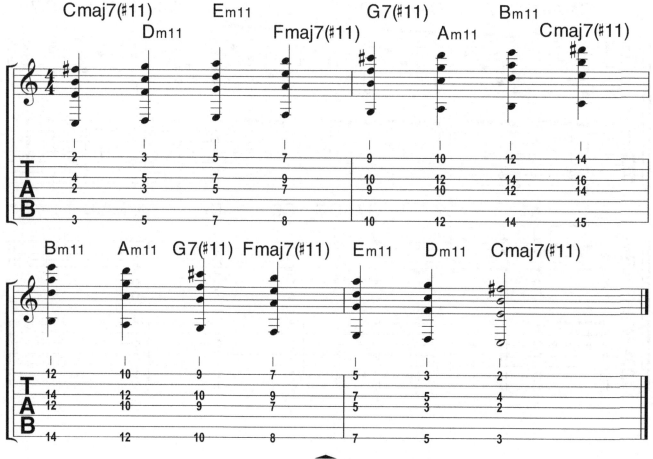

ou may also replace the 5th with a 13th. There are a couple of ways to do this. First, add diatonic 13ths to all of the chords. Notice that in some cases, rather than forming a 13th chord, this forms an inversion of a ninth chord.

Ex. 89

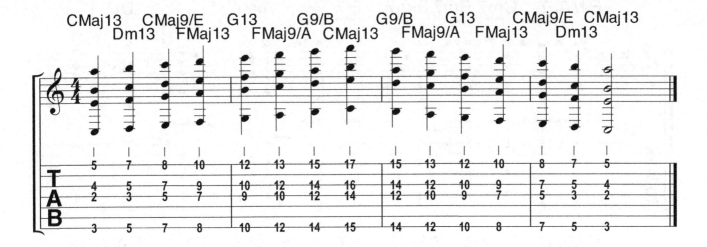

nother option you have for replacing the 5th with the 13th is to raise the 13ths when necessary, in order to make the minor chords into root position minor 13 chords.

Ex. 90

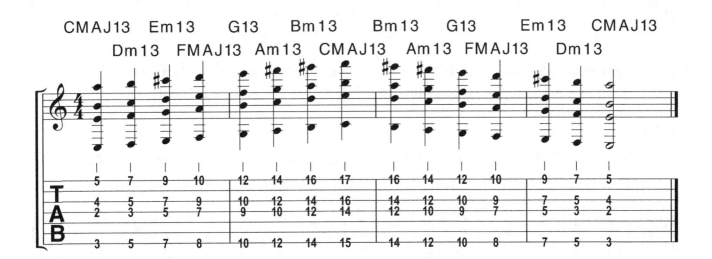

We've now added many different melody notes on the tops of these chords. Study no. 18 makes use of this in a solo context. Notice how the lower part keeps the quarter note pulse throughout.

Study No. 18 (Track 31 on CD)

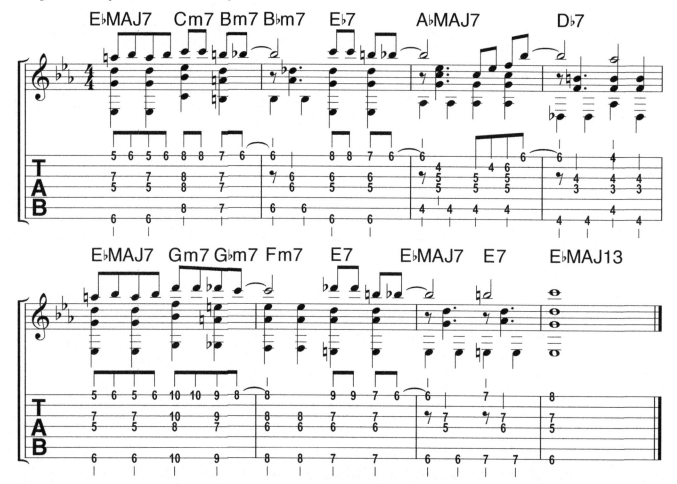

That just about exhausts the possibilities for adding notes to this voicing on the first string. So, let's look at notes we can add on the second string. We'll start by doubling the third on the second string.

Ex. 91

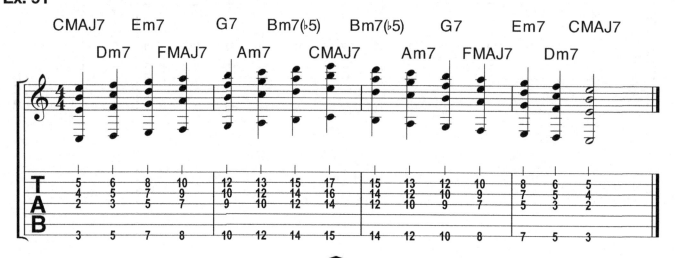

ext, instead of doubling the 3rd on the second string, add the 9th. Notice that, like the 13ths, in some cases, it is more useful to raise the 9th on the minor chords. Once again, these are very common six-string voicings, with the bass notes raised an octave.

Ex. 92

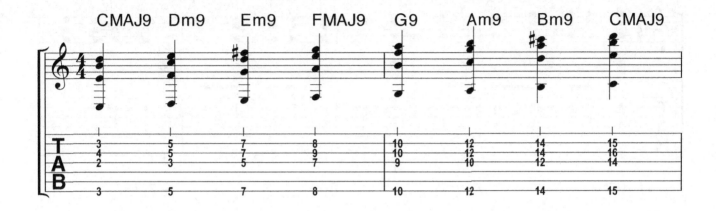

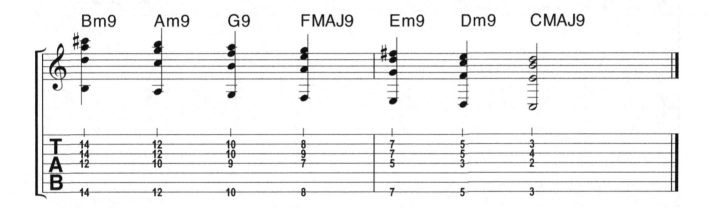

S tudy no. 19 uses these voicings as you would comping in a Latin style. Again, notice how the pulse is kept in the bottom voice, but this time in half notes.

Study No. 19 (Track 32 on CD)

The 9th may also be added on the fifth string in a lower octave. This group of voicings is particularly interesting because, even if you were to raise the bass note an octave, most of these voicings would be impossible to play on a six-string guitar.

Ex. 93

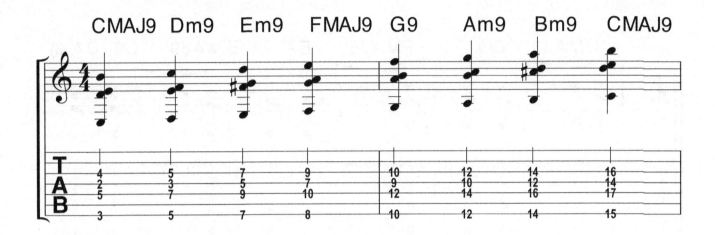

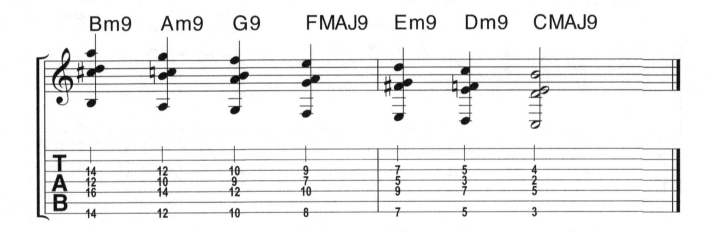

S tudy no. 20 uses these voicings in a solo context. Notice how the melody stays on the third string, and the accompanying "cluster" below. Together, this creates a very warm sound which is great for solo playing.

Study No. 20 (Track 33 on CD)

Chord Voicings II

Dropping the Seventh

In this chapter, we'll be creating a few new groups of chords by adding the 7th below the 3rd, rather than above as we did in the last chapter. Simply doing this creates a lower, warm sounding, three-note voicing that may be used for rhythm playing, comping, or harmonizing melodies where the melody note goes down to the fourth string.

Ex. 94

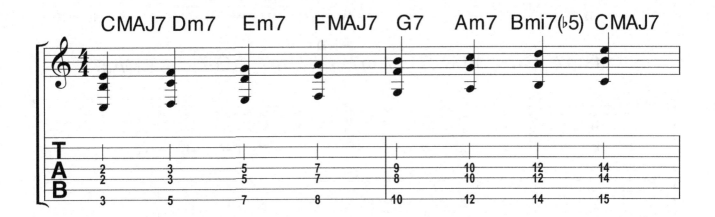

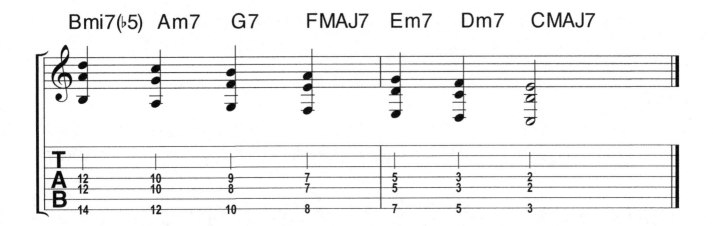

S tudy no. 21 is another rhythm guitar example, this time using these new voicings.

Study No. 21 (Track 34 on CD)

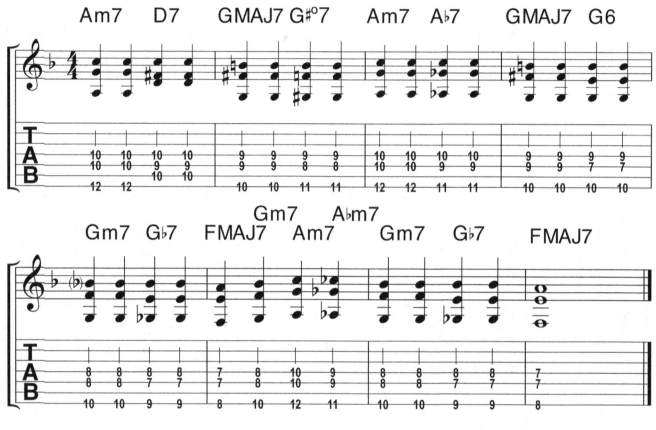

B y adding the chord fifth on the sixth string, we create a full, four note "drop-2" voicing.

Ex. 95

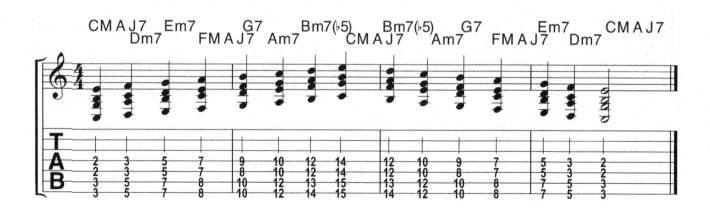

These voicings may at first sound a bit muddy, but used in context can be very effective. The next study shows how the voicings could be used as an ending. Notice that the drop-2 sound is established first in the upper register, and then carried into the lower register, moving down in a sequence. When used in this way, the voicings no longer sound muddy because the texture has already been established.

Study No. 22 (Track 35 on CD)

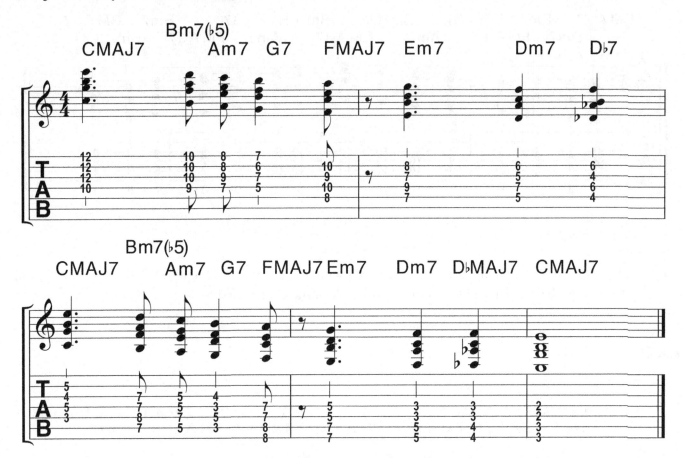

Part three - chord voicings II

By adding the 5th on the third string, we create a full, four-note drop-3 voicing.

Ex. 96

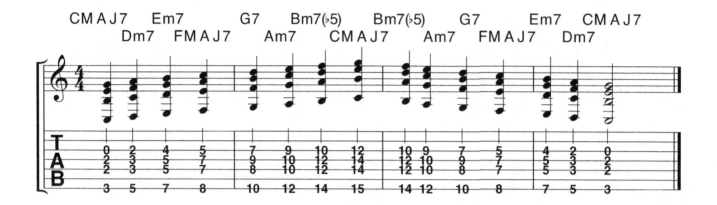

As in example 89, you may also replace the 5th with a 13th. And once again, We'll do this in a couple of ways. As before, let's add diatonic 13ths to all of the chords first.

Ex. 97

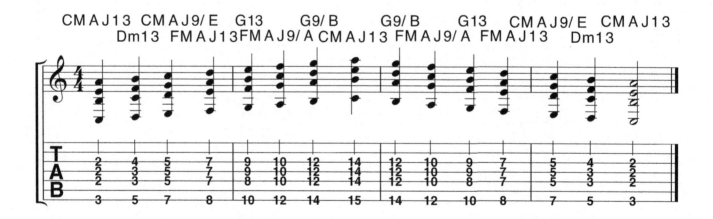

nd now for the other option: replace the 5th with the 13th, but raise the 13ths when necessary, in order to make the minor chords into root position minor 13 chords.

Ex. 98

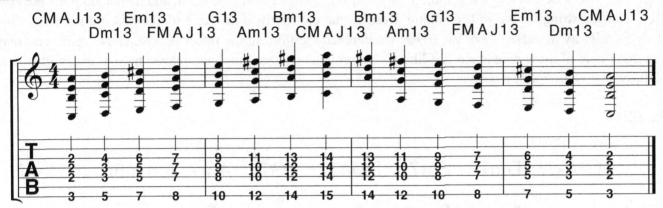

ere's another short solo example using these new chords. Play this one ballad style, somewhat freely, and notice how warm these chords sound.

Study No. 23 (Track 36 on CD)

Chord Voicings III

Raising the Third

Next, we'll be creating a few more new groups of chords raising the third, and then adding notes to the vacant strings as we've been doing. Here's what the chords look like with the raised third. Notice the similarity to example no. 91, where we doubled the third in the upper octave. Once again, you may find that many of these chords are just like six-string voicings that you have played before, except that here the bass note is dropped an octave.

Ex. 99

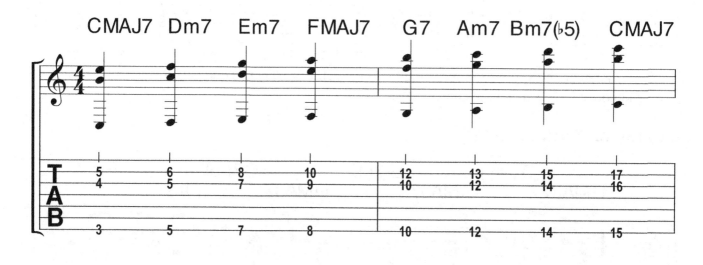

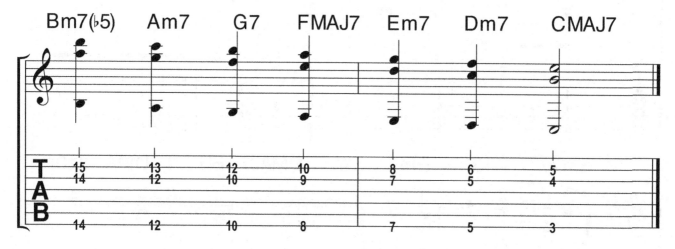

These voicings are spread fairly wide and can give the impression of two independent parts. In study no. 24, notice that the bass line is present most, but not all, of the time. This can give the illusion of a walking bass, but still allow you to phrase the melody in a musical way.

Study No. 24 (Track 37 on CD)

Part three - chord voicings III

The first note we'll add to this voicing is the 5th, first in the lowest octave. This creates a somewhat unconventional voicing. Notice the large interval in the middle of the chord. These voicings have an unusual sound to them, but still work well. The top two notes are so far away from the bottom two notes that they almost sound like two separate voicings being played simultaneously. The "open 5ths" on the bottom combine well with the "3rd and 7th" voicing on top to create an interesting effect.

Ex. 100

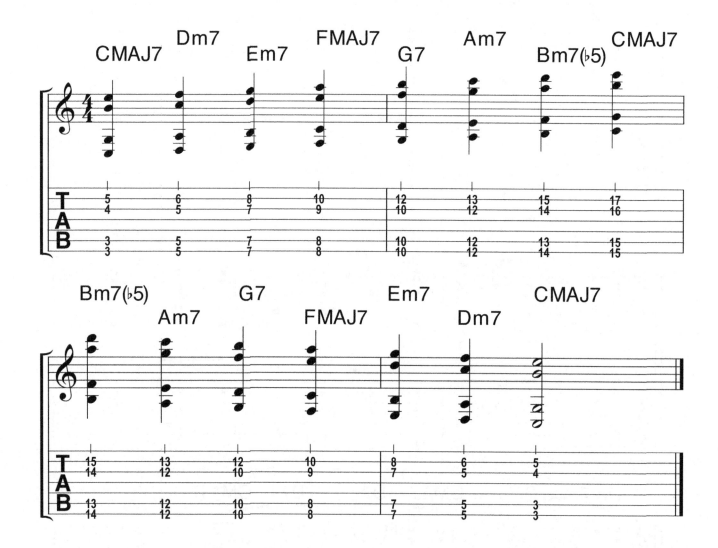

These voicings are probably best used for a special effect of some sort. In study no. 25, they are used as part of an ending. Notice how the upper two notes, and the lower two notes, sound like two independent parts.

Study No. 25 (Track 38 on CD)

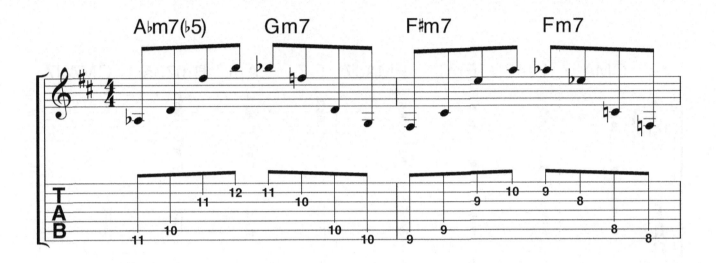

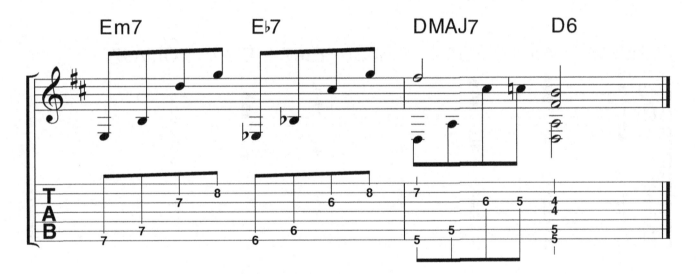

The next group of voicings adds the 5th once again, but this time up an octave on the fourth string. These voicings resemble drop-2 voicings that you may have played on the six string guitar. Now, the dropped note is dropped two octaves. This type of voicing mixes well with the type of voicing we looked at in example no. 92, as well as with six-string drop-2 voicings. You'll see this illustrated in study no. 26.

Ex. 101

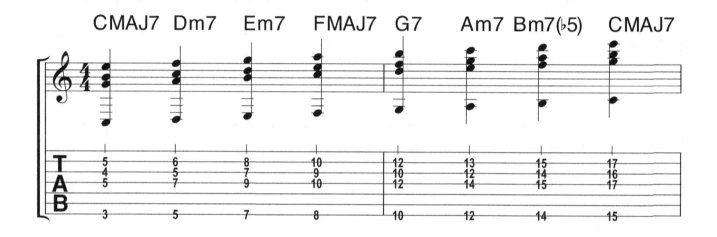

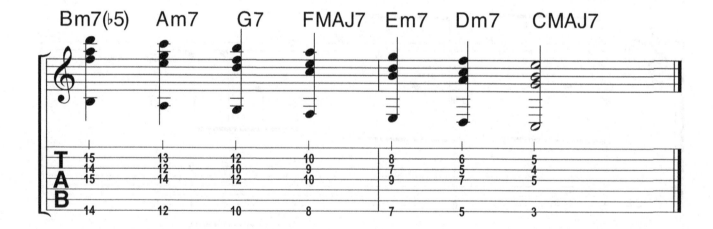

tudy no. 26 combines this voicing type with several others and illustrates how you can use them in either a solo or accompaniment setting.

Study No. 26 (Track 39 on CD)

There's one more place we can add the 5th to this basic voicing: up one more octave and on the first string. These voicings resemble drop-3 voicings. Again, the dropped note is dropped two octaves.

Ex. 102

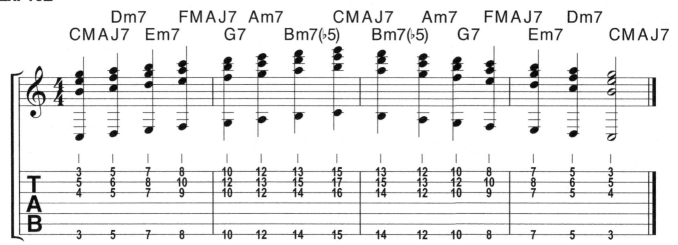

In this octave, it works well to substitute other notes for the chord fifth, like we've done in previous examples. Let's start by substituting the 11th for the 5th.

Ex. 103

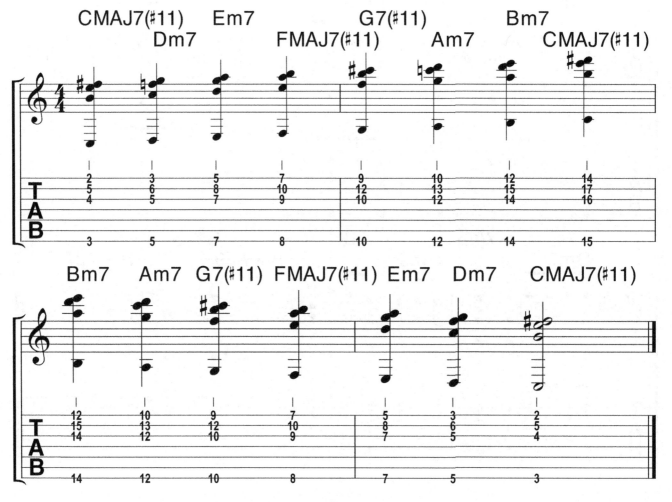

ext, we'll add diatonic 13ths to all of the chords.

Ex. 104

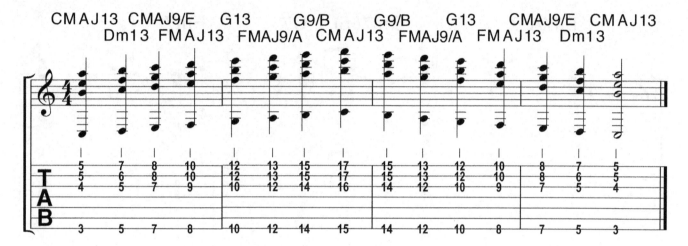

Finally, let's add a mix of diatonic and non-diatonic 13ths.

Ex. 105

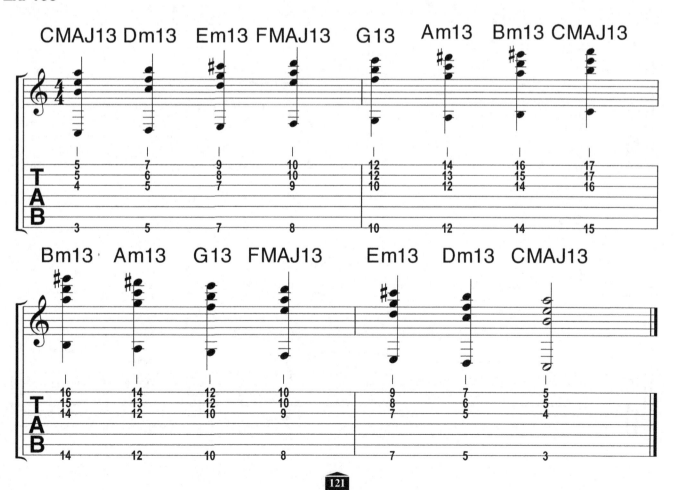

S tudy no. 27 illustrates a different type of solo playing. Notice how the bass line isn't "walking", but rather is blended into the "comping" part. This is another very effective style of solo playing, but works best when played in a very steady tempo.

Study No. 27 (Track 40 on CD)

Chord Voicings IV

Raising the Seventh

There are a couple more new groups of chords that we can create, this time by raising the 7th. These chords span nearly three octaves. Except for a few voicings that use open strings, this would obviously be quite impossible on the six-string guitar. Here's what those chords look like.

Ex. 106

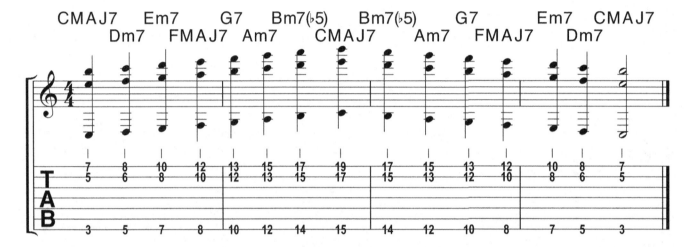

These chords are a bit awkward, so we won't be adding too much to them. However, we can add the 5th on the fourth string. Not only are these chords impossible on the six-string guitar, but they are also impossible for a good number of pianists! (Unless they have really large hands, or use their nose to play the added note.)

Ex. 107

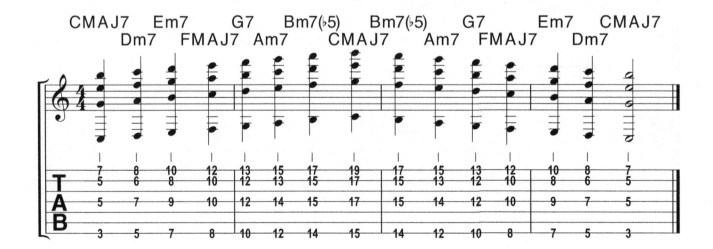

ere's another latin style comping example using these new voicings. This chord progression is commonly used as an ending.

Study No. 28 (Track 41 on CD)

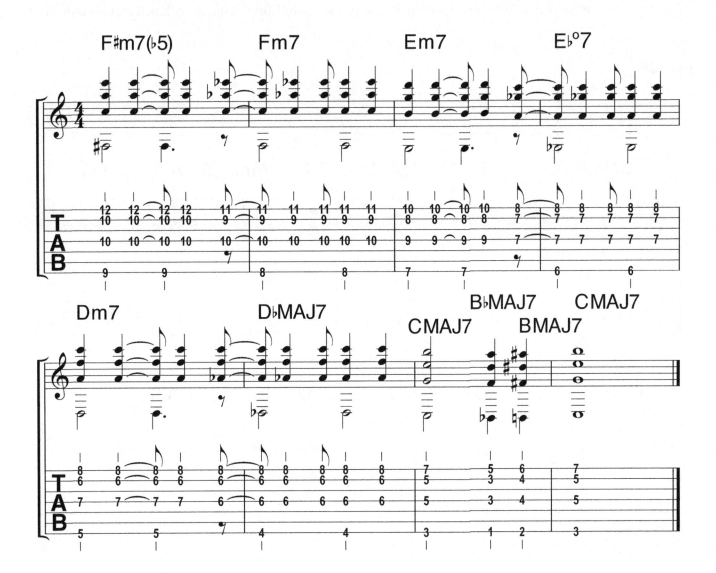

Chord Voicings V

Open Triads & Barre Chords

There are a couple more chord types left to cover. Once again, the interval of a 10th is used, but this time it is fingered a little differently. Notice that in the example below, the 10th (the 3rd an octave higher) is fingered on the fifth string. When done in this way, the chord fifth is usually included on the sixth string.

Ex. 108

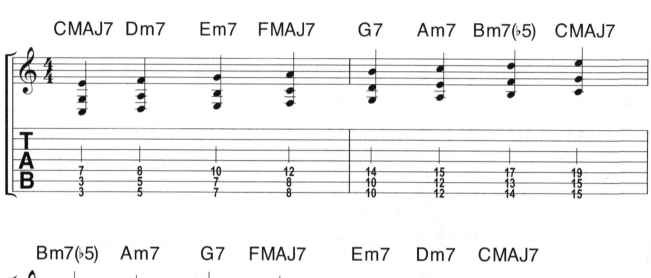

Using this fingering allows us to incorporate moving voices very easily. In study no. 29, the moving voice is first on top of the chord. In the second half of the study, notes are added above the moving voice.

Study No. 29 (Track 42 on CD)

Part three - chord voicings V

Using these chords as a base, we can form some seven-string barre chords. These very full sounding voicings are very effective in solo arrangements, ballads, intros and endings. Below are some of the more useful ones, but feel free to experiment and make up some of your own.

Ex. 109

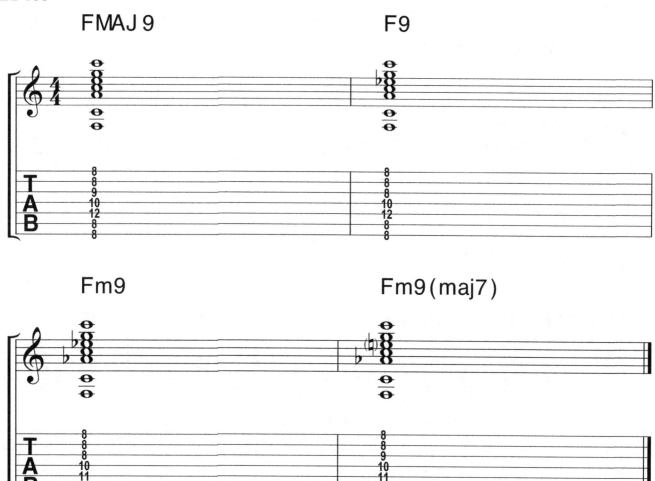

t seems fitting to end with an ending. Study no. 30 uses seven-string barre chords as you might to end a ballad. Notice that the last chord actually has seven different notes in it!

Study No. 30 (Track 43 on CD)

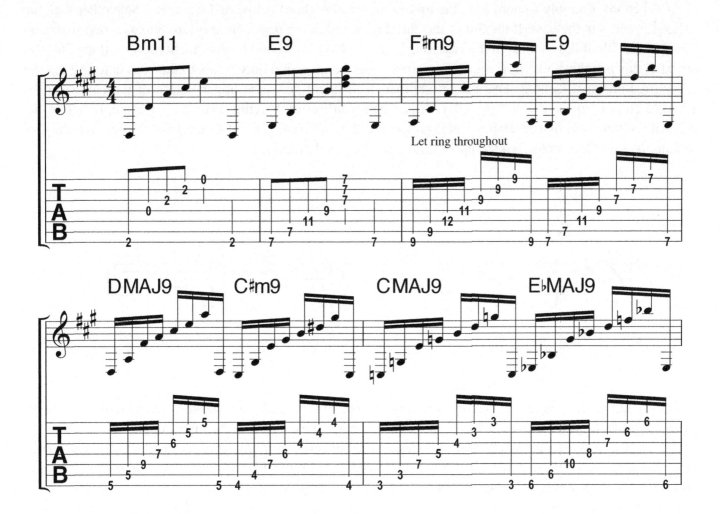

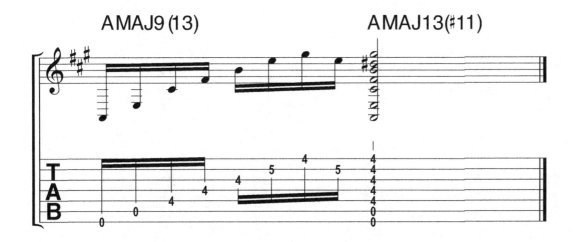

Appendix A:

An explanation of Inversions

Most of the chord voicings in this book are what are referred to as root position chords. A root position chord is simply a chord with the root in the bass. A chord is inverted when any note other than the root is in the bass. If the 3rd of the chord is placed in the bass, this is referred to as a first inversion chord. If the 5th of the chord is in the bass, this is referred to as a second inversion chord. And, if the 7th is in the bass, this is a third inversion chord. Remember that the inversion only refers to the bass note and not the upper-structure of the chord. There are a number of different ways the upper voices of the chord can be arranged (this is explained in **Appendix B: An Explanation of Voicing Types**). For example, all of the following chords are first inversion voicings because they all have the 3rd in the bass. Notice that they all contain the same four notes, but the upper voices are arranged differently.

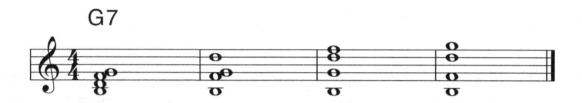

On the guitar, there are certain conventions that are generally followed when inverting a chord. Typically, you invert a chord on the guitar by moving each note in the chord up, on the same string, to the next note in the chord. If the chord has four notes in it, you can do this three times and each time will give you a different inversion of the same voicing type (the 4th time will give you the same voicing you started with, one octave higher). Of course, if you were to play the identical notes on different strings, it would still be the same inversion. But, it is recommended that you practice your inversions in string sets as shown in this example.

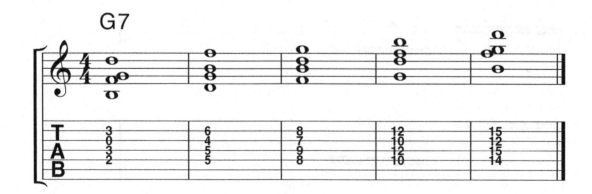

Appendix B:

An Explanation of Voicing Types

Aclose-position chord is one in which all of the notes are contained within an octave. While some close-position chords are quite playable on the guitar, many are not. The following chords are all close-position.

The terms used to describe chords which are not in close-position, describe the placement of the notes in relation to a close-position chord. Specifically, they describe which note, or notes, are "dropped" (lowered by an octave). In other words, a drop-2 voicing is one in which the second note from the top of a close position voicing has been dropped an octave. The following chords are all drop-2 voicings.

Drop-2 voicings are probably the most common guitar voicings. Also common are drop-3 voicings and drop-2 and -4 voicings.

Drop-3 voicings

Drop-2 and -4 voicings

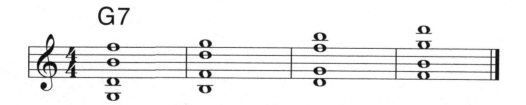

Appendix B

The added range of the seven-string guitar allows us to spread the voicings wider than usual by dropping notes two octaves instead of one. The following voicings are basically drop-2 voicings except that the dropped note has been dropped two octaves.

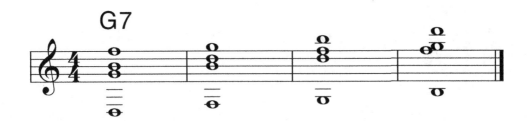

Playalong No. 1
Track 2

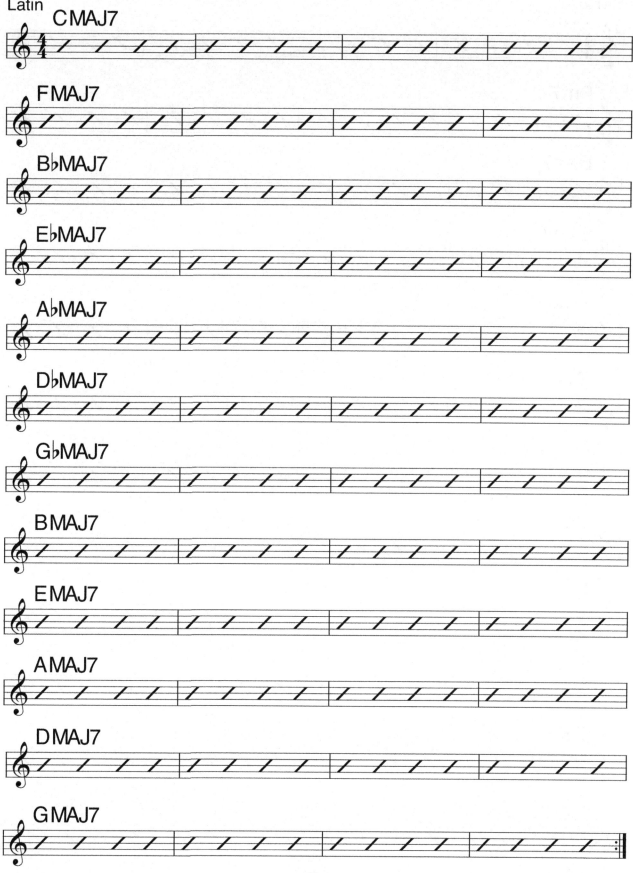

Playalong No. 2
Track 3

Playalong No. 3
Track 4

Playalong No. 4
Track 5

Playalong No. 5
Track 6

6x

Funk

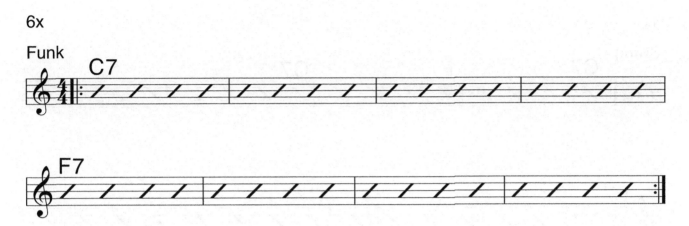

Playalong No. 6
Track 7

4x

Swing

Playalong No. 7
Track 8

Swing

| Dm7(♭5) | G7(♭9♯5) | Dm7(♭5) | G7(♭9♯5) |

| Gm7(♭5) | C7(♭9♯5) | Gm7(♭5) | C7(♭9♯5) |

| Cm7(♭5) | F7(♭9♯5) | Cm7(♭5) | F7(♭9♯5) |

| Fm7(♭5) | B♭7(♭9♯5) | Fm7(♭5) | B♭7(♭9♯5) |

| B♭m7(♭5) | E♭7(♭9♯5) | B♭m7(♭5) | E♭7(♭9♯5) |

| E♭m7(♭5) | A♭7(♭9♯5) | E♭m7(♭5) | A♭7(♭9♯5) |

| A♭m7(♭5) | D♭7(♭9♯5) | A♭m7(♭5) | D♭7(♭9♯5) |

| C♯m7(♭5) | F♯7(♭9♯5) | C♯m7(♭5) | F♯7(♭9♯5) |

| F♯m7(♭5) | B7(♭9♯5) | F♯m7(♭5) | B7(♭9♯5) |

| Bm7(♭5) | E7(♭9♯5) | Bm7(♭5) | E7(♭9♯5) |

| Em7(♭5) | A7(♭9♯5) | Em7(♭5) | A7(♭9♯5) |

| Am7(♭5) | D7(♭9♯5) | Am7(♭5) | D7(♭9♯5) |

Playalong No. 8
Track 9

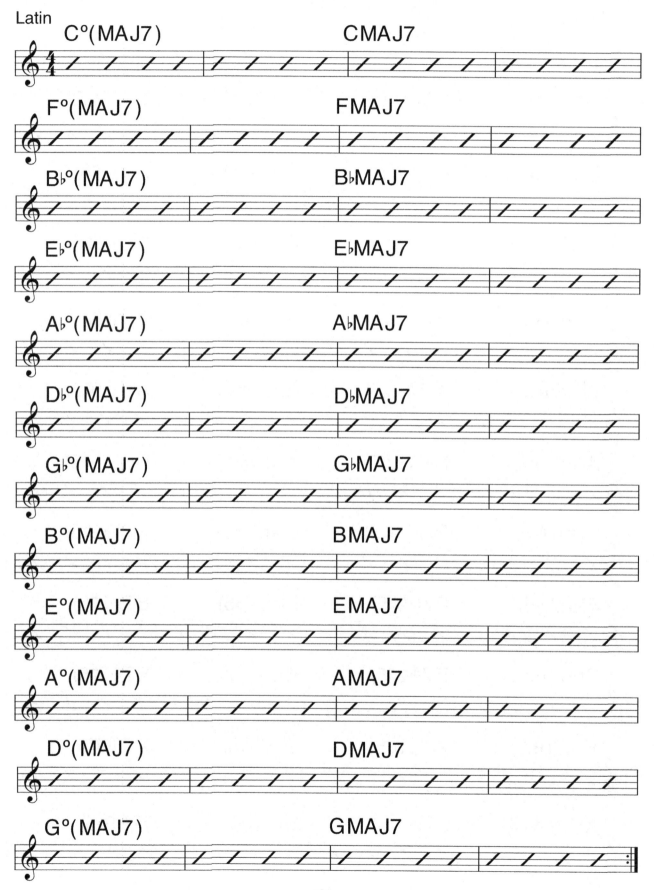

Playalong No. 9
Track 10

Playalong No. 10
Track 11

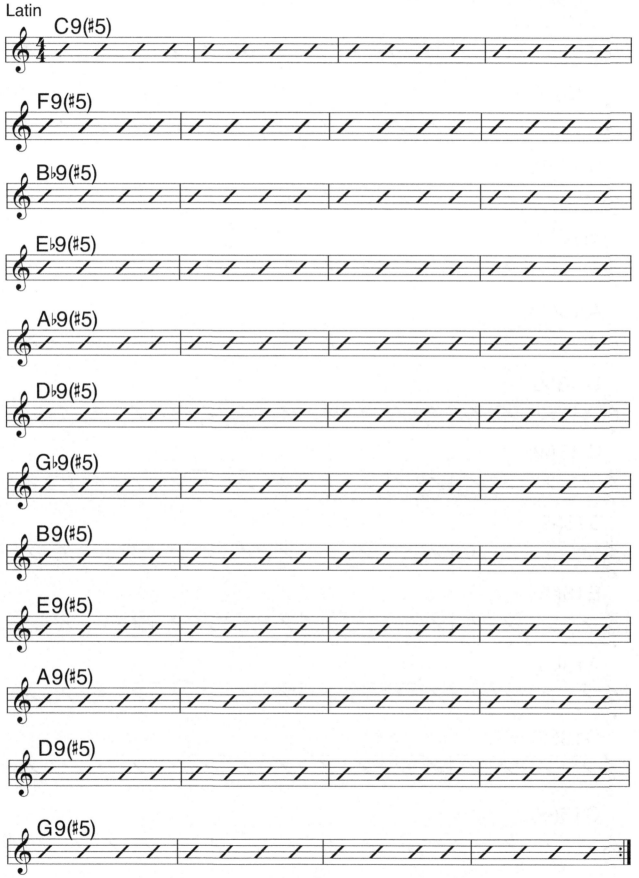

Playalong No. 11
Track 12

Playalong No. 12
Track 13

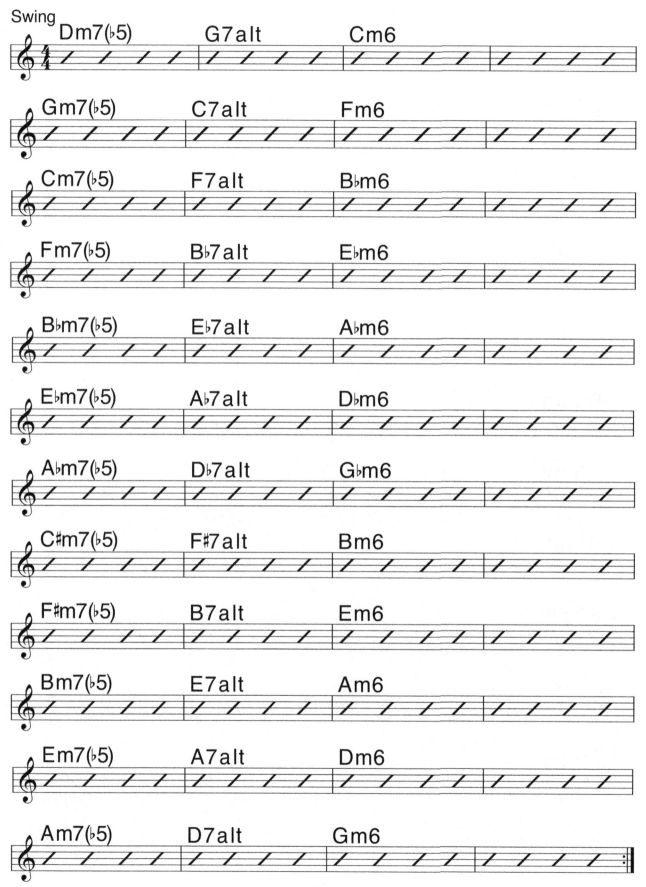

Made in the USA
Middletown, DE
09 November 2021